HEALING

for the

HEART

and the

SPIRIT

BY BRUCE PRINGLE

Produced by:
FriesenPress
Suite 300 – 852 Fort Street
Victoria, BC, Canada V8W 1H8
www.friesenpress.com

Distributed to the trade by The Ingram Book Company

TABLE OF CONTENTS

"It is a rare privilege today for the words of Proverbs 20:5 to come to life as profoundly as they have in my friendship with Dr. Bruce Pringle these past 25 years. I have kept him close as a trusted advisor and mentor and have engaged together with him in various ministry activities. In all contexts I have watched Bruce use the gifting God gave him to draw out God's purposes for individuals through wise counseling and the power of the Holy Spirit. I pray that as you read through the pages of this book, God would use these words to bring healing to you and to affirm His great purposes for your life."

Terry Mochar,
President & Founder of Mochar International

ACKNOWLEDGEMENTS

I am thankful to God who has allowed me to minister to thousands of individuals over forty years of counseling. The Holy Spirit has been the Counselor in all these times. Often I was at a loss to work through very difficult issues of brokenness, abuse, loss and grief, but God intervened.

Thank you to the many special people who chose to interact with me in counseling and received God's healing in their marriages, families, churches and their individual lives; without them this book would never have been written.

Thanks to Darlene Polachic, Karen Stiller and Willa Fernets for their journalism and editing skills that have contributed greatly to the finished project. I am thankful to the many that have encouraged me to write the book and those who have contributed as readers and financial backers.

Thank you to my sister Sharon, who shares her story of our family's brokenness through alcoholism and the horrors of an abusive foster home experience—and to my siblings who chose to follow God and receive His healing.

I am grateful to God for my family. Many times our children would take the receiver off the phone so we could have a meal in peace. There were many interruptions in our home because of individuals who needed to share their pain. My family always responded graciously.

Thank you, Coralee, for your unfailing love for your Mom and me. Thank you for the contribution to the book with the prayers and other pertinent resources within some of the chapters.

I appreciate Coralee's husband Chad and our special grandchildren Cade and Quin. Thank you Boyd and Ericka for your strength and love for your Mom and me.

I praise Almighty God for Fern, my wonderful wife of over forty years. Her enthusiasm for God's leading in the counseling ministry, her prayers and unconditional love have made me a blessed and fulfilled man.

I was nine or ten when it happened—the event that blasted open the floodgates and released the emotions bottled up inside me for all of my young life. My foster father slid off his chair and died of a massive heart attack.

What would happen to me now? All I could think about was self-preservation.

Later, on the day he died, I rode my bike through my paper route in a small Northern Ontario town. I cried so hard and trembled with such profound rage, that I had to stop pedalling. It wasn't so much that I, a welfare child in a foster home, would miss my foster father. The realization that I would have to stay in that foster home with an abusive foster mother, without the mild protection he provided, terrified me.

I was furious with God. Why hadn't He killed her instead of him? How could God take this quiet, passive man and leave his horrible, abusive wife? It wasn't fair.

"Why?" I screamed at God as I stood astride my bike, fists clenched around the handle bars, tears rolling down my cheeks. "Why didn't you kill *her*?"

The emotions I experienced as a little boy in an abusive foster home are not unique. Ours is a fallen world, full of hurt and pain, and all the destructive negative emotions they spawn. Never before in the history of North America—and indeed the world—have there been more family break-ups. Divorce is a reality in our communities like never before. Broken families are the norm now, instead of a shocking and sad exception.

Mental, physical, sexual, emotional and religious abuse is out of control. As society and educational systems can attest, there is a marked lack of restraint on children by their parents. Parents no longer control, or apparently desire to control, their children. With this lack of restraint, children and youth are experimenting more with drugs and alcohol. Violence is part of the culture.

Every day the media is rife with messages to "buy this," or "look like that," or "behave this way," because "everybody does it." The subliminal images do their work of seducing multitudes into destructive behaviours and lifestyles. Social media outlets like Facebook and Twitter mean that we are always plugged in and connected to a multitude of others. Young people face even more pressure to conform and compete.

People caught in destructive lifestyle behaviours often haul around anger, guilt, fear, rejection, loneliness, hopelessness, and a host of other damaging tendencies. These behaviours can become so all-consuming that their thinking grows clouded and confused. It becomes very difficult to break out of this vicious cycle.

In 40 years of counseling, I have seen destructive behaviours tied to past damage and abuse of some kind in a significant number of cases. Unresolved, such behaviours fester and intensify to the point where the person is affected emotionally, physically, socially, and spiritually. The downward spiral can lead to depression and ultimately, to a pit so black that suicide seems the only solution.

In the Bible, Hebrews 4:12-16 says that the Word of God is living and powerful, and describes it as sharper than any two-edged sword. That well-known passage says that God's Word is "a discerner of the thoughts and intents of the heart." No one can hide from God's sight, "but all things are naked and open to the eyes of Him to whom we must give account." But there is comfort also: "Seeing then that we have a great High Priest who has passed through the heavens, Jesus the Son of God, let us hold fast our confession. For we do not have a High Priest who cannot sympathize with our weaknesses, but was in all points tempted as we are, yet without sin. Let us therefore come boldly to the throne of grace that we may obtain mercy and find grace to help in time of need."

This passage promises that God's Word can make all the difference. It "pierces even to the division of the soul and spirit." That means the real you.

God's Word "affects the joints and marrow," the physical, "the thoughts and intents of the heart" which are the mental and spiritual parts of our beings. All of these areas impact us socially. It is critical to understand that if debilitating emotions are not dealt with, they will become strongholds—unhealthy priorities that control one's life and are not easily released.

There is hope, and there is help. No matter how difficult the circumstances you face or how impossible your life seems, you can choose how you will respond and how you will cope with your pain. Jesus Christ will give you the strength. That is what this book is about: helping people deal with and find healing from all the negative emotions that can destroy us.

I know there is genuine hope because I have witnessed it firsthand in the hundreds of clients I have counseled in my practice, but I have also found it in my own broken life when I chose to follow Jesus Christ, the source of all healing. Through Christ I received the practical tools to understand the crippling negatives in my life, and the strength to deal with them in a healthy and decisive way.

Out of my healing an overwhelming desire grew to help others find healing from their own hurts and pain. During my more than 40 years in the counseling field, I have witnessed many wounded people find freedom and deliverance.

This book will speak hope to the hopeless and healing to the wounded. It tells my personal story of brokenness and despair and explores some of the painful and destructive emotions that bound and imprisoned me. I include examples from my years in counseling. You will see that the same weaknesses and damaging tendencies that bound me are common to many others as well. In this book, you will find solid, scripture-based directions for attaining healing. The strategies offered here are practical and effective tools for overcoming the things that drag us down. Ultimately, they all point to Jesus Christ, without whom there is no real hope or healing.

"Come to Me, all you who labour and are heavy laden, and I will give you rest. Take My yoke upon you and learn of Me, for I am gentle and lowly in heart, and you will find rest for your souls. For My yoke is easy and My burden is light" (Matthew 11:28-30).

When I was four or five, I watched my father try to kill my mother.

The house we lived in was not much more than four walls and a roof with old blankets hung as room partitions. I peeked out from behind the blankets and saw my dad go after my mom. Fortunately, a visitor who was a little stronger than my dad (and a little more sober) was able to stop him.

Needless to say, ours was a very different kind of home. There were seven of us: my mom, my dad and five children. I was the fourth born.

There were always parties at our house, but they weren't fun. They involved poker games and excessive drinking. Fights broke out often. My siblings and I would get up in the morning and discover empty beer bottles, glasses, and broken debris strewn about.

My father abused alcohol and everyone around him. He was destructive in the home. Dad was a powerful man and most people were afraid of him, especially when he was drunk. As a very small boy, I witnessed my dad in a number of fights. It was not uncommon, during a middle-of-the-night poker game and drinking spree, for him to throw some other man against the wall and beat him.

My sister Sharon, the third child in our family, remembers our house burning down. I was a baby. It happened in the evening. I was in the bedroom with our mother, and Sharon and my older brothers were lying on the living room floor reading comics in front of a crackling pot-bellied stove. One of the boys happened to glance at a darkened window and saw the reflection of flames licking at the living room ceiling. Everyone rushed out into the cold winter night in their pyjamas and watched our house burn to the ground.

Even though she was only a little girl, Sharon knew that things were changing for our family after that night. There were several moves. Dad lost his job on the railroad and drifted in and out of employment. Partying and fighting became a way of life for him.

Eventually Dad walked out, leaving Mom with five small children. Because Dad was gone, Mom worked in the kitchen of a local hospital in order to support us. Of course, there were no social services in those years, and no government assistance for single mothers raising children on their own. Nor was there anyone to do child care for us while Mom worked—other than the new man who moved in with my mother (but didn't marry her).

It wasn't long before tongues wagged and fingers pointed. We had to leave town. The new man was just as abusive as my dad. He didn't take it well when Mom decided to separate from him. One night in a drunken stupor he kicked the door down and viciously beat her. I clearly remember my brothers and sister and I screaming and crying as this ex-boyfriend tried to kill her.

We moved on again.

At one point, the six of us lived in one room of a rented house. My mom cooked on a wood stove and used an outside toilet. We weren't attending school and one day, a big, burly policeman arrived at our door with a welfare worker in tow. They loaded the six of us into a car and took us to the next town.

I recall eating a dinner of cold beans from a can in the boarding house. Later in the week, we found ourselves in a courtroom where my mom was declared an unfit mother. "Mrs. Pringle," the judge said, "you're no longer fit to look after your children. We are removing them from your care."

Meanwhile, our dad was somewhere far away doing his own thing—summed up by the old cliché: wine, women and song. He was probably unaware, or maybe he didn't even care, that the family he had abandoned was torn apart.

I don't recall my mother's reaction to the pronouncement that her children were being taken from her and would become wards of the province. I'm sure she was devastated. I only know what I felt. Terror.

A family divided

My two older brothers left Ontario and travelled to Manitoba through an arrangement that may have included some relatives. They were already in their early teens and were most likely put to work. Sharon, eight, was sent to one foster home, and my younger brother and I were placed in another. I was six, my brother was five.

I have two very clear memories of our transition from the courtroom to our foster home. We ate French toast, smothered with butter and brown sugar, at a home. I had never tasted anything that delicious. I gobbled down every bite. The other memory is not so pleasant.

My brother and I were delivered to a transitional home, where we slept on a sofa. A framed picture of a very large eye hung on the wall. I suspect the artist was trying to convey the idea that the eye of God is constantly on His children, comforting and protecting them. For a confused and fearful six-year-old, there was nothing comforting about it. I didn't know much about God at that point, although I'd heard the names of God and Jesus Christ used often enough in curses. I had also heard that God would punish you if you were bad. People said He could be found in church, and because of that, I was terrified of the church in our town. Whenever I had to go near it, I would run past as fast as I could, hoping God wouldn't come out and get me.

It didn't take long, even for a six-year-old, to recognize that the home we were eventually brought to was worse than the one we'd left. The foster mother had a mean, explosive temper. Her husband was a quiet, gentle man who left the job of looking after us to his wife. Occasionally, when she was being hard on us for some simple thing, he would say, "Just leave the boys alone." Perhaps because of that, I felt we had a champion in him, if not a protector. This was the man I mourned at his death, knowing that my one adult friend was gone forever. I can hardly describe my emotions during that initial period. There was certainly bewilderment and confusion. Why had we been brought to live with strangers, and not very nice strangers, at that? Why couldn't we live with our mom? How was it that someone could just show up at your door and take you away from your mother?

Being in a different home, with a different set of parents, filled me with despair. I missed my mom terribly, and I know my brother did too. Night after night, he would sob his heart out. Our foster mother would yell, "Shut up and go to sleep!" I tried to support him as best I could, but as a six-year-old caught in my own pain, I didn't really know how.

I was filled with fear: fear of being away from my mother; from not knowing what would happen to me; and fear of this volatile woman who was now our foster mother. I recognized very early on that this new environment was not going to be kind and loving. I feared I'd never be able to get back with my mom. I was terrified I'd be in the foster home forever. I feared my foster mother's punishment. My brother and I were being spanked and slapped around, at times it seemed for no reason at all.

The fact that I was a bed-wetter deepened my terror by many degrees. Every night I went to bed petrified that I would wet the bed and be spanked. Of course, that's exactly what happened. It was a vicious circle that continued for a long time.

My brother and I were told we couldn't bring anyone into the house. Once, we were playing outside with some neighbour kids and it began to pour rain. We let the children into the house. She arrived home. The friends scattered like mice, but we were stuck, and we were punished severely.

My brother received his share of abuse. He wasn't a good reader. I believe he probably had some vision problems. I can still see her standing over him at the kitchen table screaming, "Read!"

We never knew just when we were going to be hit or slapped. Often, for no apparent reason, she would run at me and slap me hard across the head, often unexpected, often from behind. (Early on in our marriage, I told my wife never to come up behind me and grab me because my reactions are instinctive).

The foster family operated a market garden and from the very beginning, my brother and I were made to work in it. It was not unusual for the foster mother to hit us with whatever was in her hand—a knife, a hoe, a digging fork. If she had a hoe or a digging fork in her hand and noticed a potato we hadn't picked up, she would haul off and strike us with the garden tool.

We learned to get out of her way quickly if we didn't want to receive a hard whack to the head.

As very young children we washed floors, tidied the house, and carried heavy loads of wood. Today, a child who is being abused can speak up, but my brother and I lived in that foster home for ten years and not once did a foster worker, or a welfare caseworker, or a policeman ever come to check out the home. In fact, the system thought our foster mother was doing a fine job; she was considered one of their stellar foster parents. They used her again and again when children needed a home. We were told if we didn't keep our mouths shut, we'd end up in reform school. That was something we feared more than the abuse. It would appear that there were no laws in those days to protect children.

My fear of punishment extended to God. I believed God was some kind of boogeyman who couldn't wait to get you. God was the Guy in the Sky and you either lived up to His expectations or He would zap you.

I thought if you were a good person God would leave you alone, but I knew there was no way I could ever be good enough to meet God's standards.

My brother and I went to Sunday school occasionally. Any appeal it might have had evaporated the day my Sunday school teacher slapped me across the face. I was probably talking to another kid, or maybe goofing around. The teacher was growing edgy because it was near the end of the session. Perhaps he badly needed to get outside for a smoke. Years later he became my high school shop teacher. I had to deal with him, and my own issues yet again. I resented him, feared him and did not trust him, which was my standard thinking for those who were abusive while in authority.

My brother and I received no encouragement whatsoever in the foster home, and we needed it so badly. The only person I can ever recall from those years who gave me any kind of encouragement, was a schoolteacher named Mrs. Ward. She was aware of our background and was very protective of my brother and me. The two of us were forced to wear old black boots to school. The boots left marks on the hallway floors, which made the janitor very angry. He would come looking for us, but Mrs. Ward would step in and tell him to leave us alone.

My brother and I were always hungry. If I could steal some money to buy a chocolate bar, I would. Sometimes the two of us were so hungry we would sneak into the bread truck on the street and steal a sweet roll or two to eat. And self-esteem? I didn't have any. I considered myself nothing. I came from a broken marriage, a broken home, an alcoholic father, and a mother who was financially unable to care for us. It didn't matter that none of it was my doing. I had no sense of acceptance, security, or belonging. I felt totally insignificant. I was unwanted. A welfare kid no one valued. At times others made fun of me, especially over the clothes I had to wear.

Sharon's foster home was in a town nearby, and even though our foster mothers apparently knew each another, no contact or communication was allowed among our siblings. When I was about eight, a couple of our aunts picked up Sharon and brought her out to see my brother and me. Sharon's foster mother had her "all dolled up" to impress the aunts, but my brother and I were dirty and shabby. We were only given clean clothes once a week and we had to make them last. As soon as we came home from school, we had to get to work, and our work clothes were torn and ragged and dirty.

Anger builds

I punched the walls and kicked furniture. Sometimes I took it out on the other foster kids the agency brought to the home. Generally, they only stayed a few weeks at a time, but if they didn't help with the work, I threatened to beat them up.

The longer I lived in that home, the deeper my anger and resentment grew. Back then, it was directed at the policeman, the social worker, and especially at the foster mother. I blamed them for everything that was happening to us. Today, I realize my anger probably stemmed more from feeling rejected and abandoned by my parents and my resentment over my mother's inability to care for us.

In my misery, there were times when I would call out to God—the God I really didn't know—and demand to know why He had put me in another abusive home when I wasn't the alcoholic. I was not the one who had left my wife and children. But there was no answer. My sense of abandonment was deep. I wanted so much for my mother to do what she needed to do to get us back. I desperately wanted to believe that the foster home was just a temporary thing and that we would soon be back home.

That didn't happen. The longer we stayed, the deeper my sense of loss and abandonment grew.

One summer, my brother and I were sent to a church camp. Apparently the camp organizers phoned Social Services to see if any children in foster care might like to go. We, it seemed, were likely candidates. While we were at camp, Mom came by with her current boyfriend. They had already picked up Sharon, and the three of us went to spend a week with Mom and her boyfriend. I tore out of the camp dining hall and slid down the walkway railing as fast as I could.

My mother had come for me! She wanted me back! We had a wonderful week together. I was convinced this was the start of getting back with our mom. Instead, it was the last time I would ever see her. She would die in a terrible car accident with her boyfriend when I was 14. Both were drunk and killed instantly. Many years later, on my own journey of healing, I would stand at her grave and wonder about my mother and where she was at that moment.

My most profound fears were even more solidified the day my foster dad died. As long as he lived, I'd always felt that he was there to protect us. But then he was gone. I hated my foster mother from the depths of my being.

All I wanted to do was vent my anger. As I coped with this new reality, I developed a two-sided persona. I became a pleaser toward people who treated me well, but mostly I dealt with my anger by flinging myself into sports. I became driven to win. I needed to be the best in order to feel good about myself. It was the only way I had any control of my life, and I needed to feel some control because in the foster home situation, I was totally helpless.

I gained my self-esteem from pats on the back from my peer group for my sport achievements. I wasn't a good student. The only thing I liked about high school was the sports, especially football, baseball, and hockey. I also liked hanging with my friends at school. And I liked the girls.

If I won a swim race, for instance, I knew I would get some positive strokes. When I got punished at home, or criticized, I told myself I could go out and play sports and do well.

This coping strategy did not work for my brother. He was not athletically gifted, and I believe he had a harder time in school than I did. He had no outlet for his anger and negative emotions.

I'm convinced it was my lack of self-worth that fuelled my need to be number one in everything I did, whether it was swearing or swimming.

We had a lake about a hundred yards from our house, and my friends and I used to have swimming races. I was a strong swimmer and could spend two hours in the middle of the lake without my feet ever touching the bottom. We had competitions where we would find a little box turtle and take it out on the lake in an old tub of a boat we'd found adrift. We'd take turns tossing the turtle out of the boat, then diving in and swimming after it. We had to catch the turtle before it reached the mud at the bottom of the lake and bring it back to the boat for the next guy to chase. Of course, I did everything possible to catch the turtle in the fastest possible time. We spent hours doing this. When we grew tired, we released the turtle and headed for shore.

We also held competitions to see who could swim the farthest underwater. I would get my buddies to go first so I could beat the best distance and be the hero. My self-image was so crushed, I just had to win. I had to be somebody. I would sooner explode underwater than lose a race. (It wasn't often I did lose, because I had developed a different stroke—I'd swim on my side while underwater—which made me faster than the others).

Because we were welfare kids, my brother and I often were blamed for things we didn't do. We were accused of stealing some camping equipment because our names appeared on the invoices that were submitted to the welfare department. It turned out that one of our case workers with Children's Aid had ordered the camp equipment for himself and put the Pringle boys' names on the invoice.

Breaking point

I was in my mid-teens when my bitterness and antagonism in the foster home reached the breaking point. Things had been building up for years, and both my brother and I had taken about as much as we could take.

It started with the foster mother being upset about something—again. She was going to beat my brother—again. But he was fourteen or fifteen by this time and sick and tired of taking this kind of punishment. When she went to the woodbox for a piece of wood to beat him, he followed and pushed her into it. She demanded he let her up. He refused.

When her son-in-law heard about the incident, he came in to take a strip off my brother. I made a derisive sound. He jumped at me, intending to beat me senseless. He grabbed my shoulder, but I, too, had had enough.

"Get your hands off me, buddy," I snarled.

"Don't you call me buddy," he blustered.

I was so consumed with all the years of hurt and rage that I couldn't contain it any longer. In fact, I was so angry that had he taken the confrontation any further, there was no way he could have handled me. I was strong from all the hard work I'd been forced to do all my life; he wouldn't have stood a chance. I guess he recognized this, because he backed down.

Not long afterward, my brother and I were out one evening and returned a few minutes past curfew to find the door locked. That was it. The next day she told us to get out. It was one of the greatest days of my life. I was sixteen. We were in our room, packing our things, crying, laughing, and punching each another—we were like two birds being freed from their cage. The fact that we were being sent to a home for delinquents didn't take the edge off our delight.

The delinquent home was actually a receiving facility where troubled kids of all kinds were dumped off and there we waited to be picked up again. For years we'd lived in fear of being sent to the delinquent home or reform school. It was held over our heads as a threat. Now we were there, and it was great! People were kind to us. They actually seemed to care about us and showed gentleness, love and respect.

I didn't think there was too much prospect for me, a rebellious kid who'd been kicked out of the last home, to find a new foster home. Who in their right mind would take a chance and offer to look after me? I was right. My brother was moved to another foster home, but I was passed by. And passed by. Still, in that receiving home, I experienced more love in a few weeks than I had in the ten years I'd been in our foster home. So I really didn't care if anybody picked me up or not.

The long road home

As it happened, a buddy of mine from school persuaded his mother to take me in. This guy's mom was a Christian. I hadn't run into too many of those in my life. She was a teacher. Her alcoholic husband had walked out on the family and never returned. She'd raised her family on her own, and now her son begged her to take me in. She must have had some serious reservations, but at last she agreed to talk to me and see if I would be interested in staying in their home "on her terms." We sat down to talk.

"You can come into our home on one condition," she said. I was smoking and drinking and doing a lot of other things I shouldn't have been, and I expected some or all of that to figure into her requirement. I couldn't have been more surprised when she said, "The condition is that you come to church with us on Sunday mornings."

I figured that was a piece of cake—as long as somebody else woke me up. She didn't even demand I stop smoking. I could butt out the cigarette before I went inside and light up as soon as I got out again. If necessary, I could even see myself going to church with a hangover. As long as I put in my one hour of purgatory, I would be fine. If that's what would get me into a home, I could do it. No problem.

I discovered this was one of those churches where they talk about committing your life to Jesus Christ. Now that struck me as dangerous. It is one thing to talk about a God who is scary, or a God you can mention in passing when you look up into the sky or examine the dandelions.But in this church, they talked about believing in Jesus and accepting Him into your life, and letting Him change it. I expected to be preached at about smoking and drinking, but I never once heard a sermon about that. What I did hear about was having Jesus in my life.

A godly man from the church began reaching out to me and showing me love. This was a first for me. He began to challenge me to make a commitment to God. Of course, at the time, it was the last thing on my mind. Still, I kept my commitment to go to church, and things began to happen inside. I didn't feel quite as free about some of the things I was doing.

In the meantime, school wasn't going well. I was behind in my homework and had detentions to serve. And one day, at seventeen, I walked down to the office and said to the secretary, "My name is Pringle and I'm quitting school." I turned and walked out with no intention of ever going back. I was done.

Within three days I was working and doing what I needed to get myself happy again. I lived for the weekends when I played guitar and was lead singer for a dance band. The money was good. I had lots of friends. I loved the prestige, but it didn't bring me happiness or joy. It gave me an emotional kick for a few hours, but it was like a temporary upper that didn't last. Often, when I'd come home early in the morning from being on the road with the band, I'd think, 'Hey, is this all life is about?' Sometimes I'd come home with my head swimming from drinking too much alcohol, thinking: "God, if you're really there, You need to do something. Because if You don't, I've had it. If this is what life is all about, I want out."

Months later, my girlfriend graduated from high school and invited me to the ceremony. I sat in the high school gym and watched as, one after the other, the graduates shook the principal's hand and received their high school diplomas.

As I huddled in a back corner, it hit me. I would never, ever graduate from high school.

I can't describe how deeply that depressed me. I was ready to cry. I couldn't wait to get out of that room and out of my suit, and to the bottle to drown my hurt and loss.

I'd been hearing about having a relationship with Jesus Christ because a friend from church was continually challenging me to invite Jesus to take control of my life. But I didn't want anyone else controlling my life. I'd come from a childhood home where alcohol controlled our lives, then moved to a place where hatred, pain, resentment and sorrow controlled the home situation. No, I still didn't want God or anybody else controlling my life, thank you very much.

Then, when I was nineteen, a youth rally came to town. I looked forward to it because there would be young people from other provinces coming. I planned to go and look things over and check out the girls. I expected to have a good time.

Instead, I had a miserable time. The preacher kept talking about the things I'd done, and he didn't even look at me when he did it. He was from Winnipeg. At that time, the speaker Elmer Towns was not a household name, but years later he became the Dean of Faculty at Liberty University. He didn't even know my name, but it seemed like he knew everything about me.

It was at that youth rally that I gave my life to Christ and accepted Him into my life. I went to the rally because of the encouragement of a pastor friend. I suppose I went to please him, not to have my life changed. In fact, if someone would have told me I would become a believer in Christ if I went to the meetings, I would have laughed at them. The surprise came when I could not resist the power of God's Holy Spirit during the invitation song "All to Jesus I Surrender." I said, "Jesus, if You can do anything with my life, You're on. I've tried to do it on my own and I haven't done a very good job."

I committed my life to Christ just by saying, "Lord Jesus, come into my life. Take away my sin. Thank You for coming into my life and forgiving my sin. Thank You for taking control of my life." It was that simple but powerful.

What a new beginning can bring

I decided to go back to school. I chose to attend a Christian residential high school and Bible school.

Going from an abusive lifestyle to a Christian environment was a major shift for me, but I was eager and determined to live in obedience to God. One of the really difficult areas was dealing with the memory of the past abuses that had crippled me as a person. God taught me to deal with each one on my knees by my bunk in the school dorm. Daily, nightly, even in the middle of the night, I prayed to be released from my memories of the past.

The hardest thing was knowing I had to forgive the people who had hurt me. I prayed over each person and each incident. God taught me that choosing to forgive someone was something I would probably have to do again and again.

Eventually, I reached a place where I understood that there was another spiritual dimension—besides God's realm—that was controlled by another power: "In whom the god of this world hath blinded the minds of them that believe not…" (2 Corinthians 4:3). Realizing that I was confronted by Satan's lies, I was able to say, "God, I've already forgiven that person. I don't have to do that anymore. You've dealt with it in my life, and I rebuke Satan who is bringing this all back to my mind. I resist it."

Though I had accepted Christ into my life and knew I was entirely spiritually clean, there were hundreds of things from my past that rose in my mind. I knew God was bringing them because He wanted to forgive me for each of those specific things. Dealing with my past sins mentally led to a deep emotional healing.

In grade eleven Bible class we started scripture memorization. Claiming the scriptures I was memorizing was a huge part of my healing. In one class we had to memorize John 3. The next year, it was the book of Philippians. Other scripture memorization came from reading through the Bible. When a verse jumped out at me, I'd write it down and work on memorizing it. I found myself claiming and reflecting on those verses over and over again. Having the Word of God in my mind and at my fingertips was a weapon against the Enemy. When Satan tried to make me doubt my right to serve Almighty God because of the filth in my early life, I was able to draw on scripture to fight back.

I completed my high school, and then took three years of Bible school training. I also met my wife Fern. After we married, I went on to attend university, received a Bachelor of Education, a Master of Education and a Doctorate in Counseling and Administration. In 1975, I established Christian Counseling Services in Saskatoon, Saskatchewan, along with other Christian business men. A few years later we added a Christian adoption service. I directed Christian Counseling Services for 25 years.

One year, Fern and I were in British Columbia around New Years, and I arranged to see my Dad who had been living there for some time. I had not seen him for 18 years. Because I was coming to visit, he'd made a resolution not to drink any alcohol that day. As we spent time together, it became very obvious he wouldn't be able to hold to it. Throughout our conversation, he drank more and more. Dad had friends there who were drinking heavily, too.

We talked about his life. He spoke of the waste, the disappointments with work and his relationship with his first wife (who was my mother), his second wife, and the woman with whom he lived.

It hurt me deeply that even though Mom wasn't present to defend herself, Dad made snide remarks about her and maligned her for the sort of wife and mother she was. During our time together, I tried to talk about the spiritual dimension of his life, but he would have none of it.

My dad died a few months later. He had chronic emphysema, and had been warned by his doctor that he must stop drinking and smoking.

Prior to his passing, he'd said to my oldest brother, "Whatever you do, don't let them burn me." He didn't want to be cremated. Perhaps he thought that, somehow, after he died and got into the presence of God, he would have a chance of 'making it,' if he still had a body. Perhaps because he had connived, manipulated, and controlled things in life he thought he could do the same in death.

My brother said, "Don't worry, Dad. I'll look after it." Death, however, can be ironic.

Somewhere during the process of transferring the body to the morgue and the funeral home, there was a mix-up and my dad was cremated. His body was burned. When my brother went to make the funeral arrangements he discovered the body had already been cremated and the ashes spread. We have no idea where.

This was particularly difficult for my eldest brother who had made that vow to carry out Dad's last request. This led him and his wife into more heavy drinking which would eventually cause both of their deaths, a tragic example of the powerful impact of generational sins, a deadly vice handed down like an ugly heirloom.

What do you do with all the memories of the past? What do you do with the people who abused you? What do you do with people you've witnessed trying to kill somebody you love?

What do you do with all those memories?

I knew that if God didn't heal me from my background, I would never make it in life. But God, in His great mercy, began to do just that. Little by little, He made me whole from the inside out.

Having Christ in my life made all the difference. It was Jesus Christ who got me through all the pain. It was Jesus Christ who set me free.

What about my anger and bitterness toward my foster mother? I'll be honest. There was a time when if I'd seen her dead on the floor, I've have rejoiced, clapped my hands, and shouted, "Hallelujah!" (even though I didn't know what that word meant back then). But when I gave my life to Jesus, He changed me. I've forgiven my parents for their lives of alcoholism. I've forgiven the welfare society, the social workers, and others in the system for what they did to me.

In fact, it is exactly because of everything in my life that I have had the opportunity to stand before thousands of people all over North America and declare from personal experience that it doesn't matter what your journey has been, we have a God big enough to minister to every need. Over the years, I returned to Ontario a number of times and met with my foster mom.

Because Christ wiped the bitterness from my heart, I was able to put my arm around her, give her a kiss, and say, "Mom, how're you doing?" That was not Bruce. It was Jesus. That's what Jesus can do in a person's life. I know, because He did it for me.

Chapter 2: The Evil Twins of Rejection and Abandonment

"I wish you were the one who died."

The words came from Charlotte, who had come to my counseling office for help. Charlotte was quoting her father. He spoke the hurtful words to her many years ago, following the death of her younger sister. Charlotte had lived all her adult life feeling rejected, abandoned, and lacking value in her father's eyes. He was critical of everything she did. Charlotte needed professional help. That's what brought her to my office.

One child being favoured over another is just one life experience that can lead to feelings of rejection and abandonment. These emotions are virtually unavoidable in cases of family break-up and divorce. When one person walks out saying, "I don't love you anymore," not only does the spouse feel rejected and abandoned, so do the children in the family.

As a high school teacher, I led a class discussion based on a unit relating to alcohol dependency (about which I knew a great deal). I encouraged the students to discuss what happens in situations where there is alcohol abuse in the home. As the students began sharing their thoughts and ideas, one girl ran out of the room crying. She returned later to apologize and explain that her father was a travelling salesman and a philanderer with a woman in every port. The girl's mother felt so rejected by his infidelity that she had resorted to drugs and alcohol to numb her feelings.

"I'm so confused," the girl sobbed. "Who am I, and how can I live with this?"

I think of Moira, a woman in her thirties who also felt rejected and abandoned. A homemaker who now worked part-time as a sales clerk, Moira grew up in a Christian home where she had known love and security. In her marriage however, she experienced rejection and severe loss of self-esteem because of her husband's selfish, demanding behaviour. Though he claimed to be a Christian, he was very cruel to Moira. She came to my office as a person feeling rejected in her own home, with a husband who didn't appreciate her. As we worked through her issues, I was able to help Moira see that her husband had brought a lot of baggage into their marriage. I helped her change her focus to the love God has for her, and the love of her Christian parents.

What is rejection and abandonment? Consider this illustration. As Neil took his place at the end of the assembly line for auto parts, he thought of his rise in the company to quality control manager. Yes, he had the responsibility of declaring the part fit or unfit for the auto maker. Vicky, his lovely wife of two years, was proud of Neil's hard work which had now been rewarded with an excellent promotion. Two summers ago, Vicky and Neil had said those words of commitment, "For better or for worse," expecting to honour their vow.

Neil was startled back to his senses as he noticed the movement of the conveyor belt in front of him. He could see the defective part coming slowly towards him. As he threw the damaged part into the bin labelled Rejects, Neil felt just like that defective piece. He felt sorrow and frustration at being cast off and thrown away as useless. Vicky and Neil had been happy in their love until the young engineer joined the company. Vicky had recently told Neil that she didn't love him anymore. When Vicky returned to pick up her last few things, it was almost more than Neil could take. Rejection was the most painful experience he had ever felt.

What was Bert thinking when he walked out on Marie and her five children to never return? Only of himself. Abandoned, deserted, and separated forever, with no bread-winner, with no place to call home, what a dilemma for Marie! Eighteen years later, as Bert sat in his shabby rented suite in Victoria, he cried because of the past. He was sad, but unrepentant because he blamed his wife—my mother—for the separation. I had not seen Bert (my dad) for those eighteen years, and he had never tried to contact me.

But I had been blessed to be adopted by my Heavenly Father (Psalm 27:10). Jesus Christ had saved me from all my sins and made me a new creation in Christ (2 Corinthians 5:17). I forgave my Dad for abandoning us. I had only pity towards him.

Feeling rejected and abandoned often generates other negative and destructive emotions. An abandoned individual may feel fearful and angry. They may respond with one of the stress responses known as fight, flight or freeze.

Fight is the stress response which says, "I have had enough of your anger, abuse, put downs and I will react in a verbal or physical way to stop you hurting me."

Flight is the stress response that motivates a person to leave the unpleasant situation immediately.

Freeze forces the person to be immobilized. They are unable to protect themselves by fighting back or running from the impending doom, so they remain in the unpleasant place facing their foe frozen in fear.

My brother's response to circumstances in our foster home was flight. He backed into himself and became ever more reclusive as the foster home situation worsened. I chose fight.

I grew angry and attacked. I poured myself into physical activity and sports where I was aggressive and competitive. My complete healing was yet to come.

Words can hurt

The words we speak can be almost as damaging as physical abuse. Parents, especially, can do lasting damage to their children when their words are cutting or critical. Phrases like "You'll never amount to anything," or "Why can't you be more like your sister?" create a profound sense of rejection, and of not measuring up to expectations.

In my counseling, I have seen many receive emotional healing as Christ removes the sting, the pain of those kinds of hurtful statements. You will read examples of that healing throughout this book.

This poem by an anonymous writer aptly demonstrates the two approaches parents can adopt in dealing with their children.

Which Parent are You?

"I got two As," the small boy cried;
His voice was filled with glee.
His father very bluntly asked,
"Why didn't you get three?"
"Mom, I've got the dishes done,"
The girl called from the door.
Her mother very calmly said,
"Did you sweep the floor?"
"I've mowed the grass,' the tall boy said,
"and put the mower away."
His father asked him with a shrug,
"Did you clean off all the clay?"
The children in the house next door
seem happy and content.
The same things happened over there,
but this is how it went.
"I got two As," the small boy cried.
His voice was filled with glee.
His father very proudly said,
"That's great! I'm glad you belong to me."
"Mom, I've got the dishes done,"
The girl called from the door.
Her mother smiled and softly said,
"Each day I love you more."
"I've mowed the grass," the tall boy said,
"And put the mower away."
His father answered with much joy,
"You've made my happy day."
Children deserve a little praise
For tasks they're asked to do.

If they're to lead a happy life,
So much depends on you.

Rejection and abandonment in the Bible and what God did about it

The Bible offers us several examples of rejection and abandonment, along with God's loving intervention in the circumstances.

The first is the classic example of Hagar and her son Ishmael, the child born to Abraham as a result of Abraham and Sarah's impatience and lack of trust in God's promise.

In Genesis 16 we read how Sarah (then named Sarai) tries to bring God's promise to fruition by taking matters into her own hands. She suggests that Abraham sleep with her Egyptian servant girl Hagar. Abraham agrees. Hagar becomes pregnant and bears Abraham a son whom he names Ishmael.

Fourteen years later, at God's appointed time and in Sarah's very old age, Isaac is born. That's when things get complicated. In Genesis 21: 8-21 we read that Sarah requested that Abraham send Hagar and Ishmael away. "Therefore she said to Abraham, 'Cast out this bond-woman and her son; for the son of this bondwoman shall not be heir with my son...'" (Genesis 21:10).

And so, "...though the matter was very displeasing in Abraham's sight because of his son....Abraham rose early in the morning and took bread and a skin of water and putting it on her shoulder, he gave it and the boy to Hagar and sent her away..." (11, 14).

Bewildered, rejected, and abandoned, mother and son headed south-ward and wandered in the Wilderness of Beersheba. How confusing this must have been for both Hagar and Ishmael. Abraham was a wealthy man with many servants; it wasn't like he couldn't afford to support the two of them. It's very easy to imagine Ishmael asking his mother, "Doesn't Daddy love me any more?" For fourteen years, he had enjoyed a position of privilege as Abraham's only son. Now, suddenly, he is unwanted. Abandoned. Rejected. Sent away to die. Or so he thought.

We know that God heard Ishmael's sad questions and Hagar's hope-less, helpless cries. In Genesis 21 we read: "And God heard the voice of the lad. Then the angel of God called to Hagar out of heaven, and said to her, 'What ails you, Hagar? Fear not, for God has heard the voice of the lad where he is. Arise...for I will make him a great nation'" (Genesis 21: 17, 18).

I can't count the number of times I've heard clients recounting events from childhood and saying, "Well, he or she was the favourite in our family." The unhappy result of favouritism is that those less favoured feel abandoned, rejected, less valuable and less loved.

Perhaps the best Biblical example of rejection and abandonment is Joseph, the second youngest son of Jacob. The lesson is so important that it takes up ten entire chapters in Genesis.

Joseph's older brothers hated him. Some might excuse them because Jacob made it perfectly obvious that Joseph was his favourite. His justification was that Joseph was "the son of his old age" (Genesis 37:3).

Not a good excuse.

To demonstrate his favouritism, Jacob gave Joseph a rare and beautiful multi-coloured coat. The older brothers hated Joseph more. In fact, every time they saw The Favourite wearing his lovely coat, their hatred grew.

There was another problem. Joseph was spoiled, and he was a tattler. Whenever the other boys did something they shouldn't, Joseph ran to tell their father.

Joseph was also a dreamer. Dreaming is not a problem in itself. If Joseph had kept his dreams to himself, things might have gone along quite differently. But in his conceit and arrogance, the favoured teen predicted that everyone in his family would one day bow down to him.

Hearing things like that can really bother a person. It certainly bothered Joseph's brothers, to the point where one day, when Joseph came out to the sheep pasture to check up on his siblings, they decided to teach their darling little brother a lesson. They grabbed him, ripped off his beautiful multi-coloured coat, and threw him in a well. The good news is it was a dry well. The bad news is they intended to leave him there to die.

Reuben, older and perhaps saner, planned to go back later and haul his brother out, but a caravan of Ishmaelite traders bound for Egypt happened by. The rest of the boys sold Joseph to them for twenty shekels of silver.

It isn't difficult to imagine Joseph crying. Begging. Pleading with his brothers not to let these strangers take him away. Talk about rejection and abandonment. Joseph's own brothers hated him. He was at the mercy of slave traders whose language and culture he couldn't understand. And every step of the camel's hooves carried him further and further away from the father he would most likely never see again.

The wonderful culmination to Joseph's story is that Joseph trusted God, despite terrible loss and suffering. In some ways, the account of his life that we read in Genesis 39 and onward is like a roller-coaster: sold as a slave into Potiphar's household, yet he rises to the position of manager; wrongly accused of rape and imprisoned for years; eventually put in charge of all the prisoners; released in order to interpret Pharaoh's disturbing dreams; and finally, put in charge of a contingency plan to save Egypt from coming famine.

Ultimately, Joseph was made prime minister of Egypt and saved the lives of his father and brothers. Because of his unwavering faith in God, he was able to see God's hand in all that had befallen him. Genesis 45: 5-8 is Joseph's statement to his brothers: "But now, do not therefore be grieved or angry with yourselves because you sold me here; for God sent me before you to preserve life... So now it was not you who sent me here, but God...."

Not everyone who experiences rejection and abandonment endures such dramatic circumstances as Joseph or Ishmael. Sometimes the rejection comes from a sense of inadequacy because of looks or physical limitations, or perhaps a lack of athletic ability. It can be devastating for a young person to be told they can't play on the team because they're not as good as someone else. On the playground, young girls often exclude other girls from playing with the group.

The sense of abandonment is never stronger than in cases of abuse, a subject we will discuss at length in Chapter 10.

However your sense of rejection and abandonment occurs, it can lead to feelings of low self-worth, anger and resentment, worries, doubts and fears. Low self-worth can lead to such a deep sense of inferiority and worthlessness you can wish you had never been born.

Where rejection and abandonment can lead

Depression is always a factor for those who feel rejected and abandoned. As we look at the case study of Hagar and Ishmael, it is clear that Hagar was depressed as she sat with her son in the desert. She was overwhelmed with the hurt and pain and rejection from both Abraham and Sarah.

Hand-in-hand with rejection comes self-condemnation. The self-hatred may be because we couldn't change a situation, or because of guilt. In most cases, the guilt is not real. It is false guilt which comes from others putting us down, condemning, or defiling us.

There may also be false guilt which comes from the Enemy (Satan), who generates all things negative in our lives.

A 40-year-old man came to me for help. Daniel was married, had two children, and ran a successful business. He was crippled by guilt. Daniel was made to feel deeply inferior at home. He had low self-esteem and was filled with bitterness and anger.

When he was fourteen, Daniel saw his father try to kill his mother. He shouted at his father, "I hate you! I wish you were dead!"

The very next day, the father was driving home from work and was hit broadside by a drunk driver. He was killed instantly.

Daniel, though now a grown man, was riddled with guilt. He often woke up in a cold sweat from a recurring dream where he heard himself shouting, "I hate you! I wish you were dead."

Then he sees the impact of the two vehicles colliding.

Since the age of fourteen, this man suffered under a load of false guilt, believing that he was somehow responsible for his father's death. It was a lie placed in his tortured mind by Satan, the Enemy, whom Jesus called a thief and a liar. "The thief does not come except to steal, and to kill, and to destroy" (John 10:10b). Satan makes condemning statements to us. When we listen to Satan's accusations, we become subjective and introspective about what has taken place, and we run ourselves down.

True guilt, on the other hand, can be called spiritual guilt, because it results from the Holy Spirit ministering to us. The hallmark of true guilt is the kindness and gentleness with which the Holy Spirit points out the sins in our lives. The Holy Spirit urges us to ask forgiveness from a holy God. And, as God's Word says, "If we confess our sins, God is faithful and just to forgive us our sins and to cleanse us from all unrighteousness" (John 1: 9). As well, "There is therefore now no condemnation to those who are in Christ Jesus" (Romans 8:1a).

Rejection often manifests itself in negative attitudes and reactions toward one's parents and others. If divorce, separation, or adoption are involved, there may be resentment, bitterness, or an ongoing failure to communicate. Distrust of others and rebellion against authority are also common. Those who experience rejection have a hard time trusting, and this causes difficulties in a marriage relationship. Though those feeling rejected may hear their partner saying, "I love you and I care for you," they have a hard time believing it, because of what happened in their past.

Those who struggle with rejection exhibit an inability to express love because they have never learned love or received genuine love themselves. That is why verses about God's love are so important and helpful in ministering to those who are struggling:

"For God so loved the world that He gave His only begotten Son, that whoever believes in Him should not perish but have everlasting life. For God did not send His Son into the world to condemn the world, but that the world through Him might be saved. He who believes in Him is not condemned; but he who does not believe is condemned already, because he has not believed in the name of the only begotten Son of God" (John 3:16-18).

"Who shall separate us from the love of Christ? Shall tribulation, or distress, or persecution, or famine, or nakedness, or peril, or sword? ...For I am persuaded that neither death nor life, nor angels nor principalities nor powers, nor things present nor things to come, nor height nor depth, nor any other created thing, shall be able to separate us from the love of God which is in Christ Jesus our Lord" (Romans 8: 35, 38, 39).

Some children—and even adults—adopt the attitude of: "You rejected me, therefore I will reject you." Perhaps they demonstrate their rejection by sharing little of their time. A good example is children who refuse to come home when a parent is dying because they felt rejected in their youth.

This, of course, only generates more difficulty and negativity.

For some there may be verbal acceptance, but emotional rejection. Frank's dad would brag about his son because he was very athletic, however Frank rarely saw his dad at any of his sports events or even his graduations. The emotional rejection that Frank felt from his father would fester within him for years. Later in his marriage, Frank resorted to verbal and physical abuse to vent his inner rejection and hostility that he held towards his father.

Others simply refuse to communicate. Their behaviour creates a vicious cycle. Instead of dealing with the hurt of the past, they continue to pass it on to their children. Vera came from a very strict, religious home, devoid of love, gentleness and encouragement. Her opinions were met with a negative, condescending response. Soon, Vera realized that being quiet was her safety net. She used it to perfection. Now, years later, her husband Dave and her children were impacted by Vera's inability to communicate. They were experiencing the same types of rejection that Vera had faced.

I believe that there are many like Vera, who struggled in a family, but can be released from the pain of rejection by an encounter with the Lord Jesus Christ.

I continually sought attention to compensate for my own sense of rejection and abandonment when I was young. Some of the things I did to gain attention created problems for me and for others. I tried too hard to please and struggled with accepting love because I was programmed to expect rejection. This can be a self-fulfilling prophecy.

I think of Tyler, a seven-year-old boy I counseled who struggled to deal with his parent's marital breakdown. By the time I saw him, they were divorced, and the boy's relationship with his dad was very poor. The father lived out of province and sent no support. He had absolutely no interest in his son. Tyler was repeating grade one, because he didn't care about anything.

His teacher didn't know what to do with him. Tyler was extremely frustrated and insecure, and unable to cope. He was angry most of the time, frustrated with relationships in school and with his friends. He was deeply despondent and had a very miserable self-image. Tyler felt guilty (false guilt) because he was angry at his father's lack of communication. He was also angry at his mom because she couldn't do anything about the situation. Tyler was angry at everyone else because his trust was destroyed when his dad left.

Tyler's mother brought him to our counseling agency to see if we could deal with some of her son's hurts and pain. It was very important to begin by talking about his relationship with God and Jesus. Children understand God as well as they understand rejection. At the same time, I counseled the mother to determine where she was spiritually.

I knew it was as important for the mother to work with this child as it was for me. I also contacted his teachers so we would be able to work together and help this boy with his pain and rejection.

The Distinct Case of Adoption

It is not uncommon for adopted children to experience a sense of abandonment and rejection. I think of Rodger, a man in his fifties who came into my counseling office. Married with children, he was a successful store owner in a large center. But he struggled with his worth. Rodger was adopted as a child and felt insecure all his life. He was from a home that claimed to be Christian, but was very legalistic, cruel, and at times, even destructive. Rodger never sensed any love, and even though he now had a good marriage, he still felt unloved.

As far as others were concerned, Rodger seemed to be doing very well. As I counseled him, I learned he had thought about suicide a number of times. He had such low self-esteem that he believed suicide was the only answer to release him from the rejection he'd experienced all his life. Rodger felt inferior to everyone else and resented his adoptive parents.

This man needed to embrace the reality that, as a Christian, he had a new relationship with God and with Jesus Christ. Jesus came to take away his insecurity and make him know he is profoundly important.

I encouraged Rodger to study Romans 8 and Psalm 139, which clearly describe God's love for him. As this man began to forgive others, he was able to see himself as God saw him, a person of infinite worth. As Rodger released his feelings of being rejected and abandoned by his birth parents, and resentment for the way he was treated by his adoptive parents, he began to grow in his relationship with Christ.

Later, Rodger sent me a special note stating how grateful he was to God for releasing him from his feelings of abandonment.

In my counseling practice, I have dealt with many clients who were either adopted or have adopted children. The difficulties generally arise when adoptees reach the teenage years and want to search out their birth parents.

In one case, the adoptive mother was almost paranoid and was determined to do everything she could to prevent her adopted daughter from searching out her birth parents. The more determined the child was, the more serious the conflict became.

In cases like this, I try to appeal to the adoptive parents on their own, without the child present. I encourage them to allow, and perhaps even help, the child find their birth parents. Some have done that, with mixed results. Occasionally, there is a happy and joyful reunion and relationships are established in adulthood. There is also every chance the response will be: "Don't call me again; I don't want to have anything to do with you. I'm happily married with three kids. Stay out of my life." Christian leader Bill Gothard, founder of the Illinois-based Institute in Basic Life Principles, offers some insights into the emotional difficulties and conflicts that can occur in adoptive situations. He says these conflicts generally develop in the teenage years, and may be complications for the child or the adoptive parents. (For a detailed discussion on the subject, check out Bill Gothard materials at www.billgothard.com).

- Adoptive parents have the idea the child they've been given is a blank sheet. They are not prepared to deal with child's inborn weaknesses and tendencies.
- Adopted children have greater conflicts because they struggle with a deep sense of rejection, and are more sensitive to rejection.
- When they want to find their natural parents, adopted children often have conflicting loyalties because they know it may very well hurt their adoptive parents.

It has been my experience with those with these painful conflicts, that the antidote for the rejection is spiritual acceptance. Once the individual understands that God loves them and they make a commitment to accept His love and forgiveness, the painful emotions from rejection begin to diminish. They must be taught that this response to God must first be initiated in the will by faith.

Whether a person's sense of rejection and abandonment comes from being adopted, from circumstances in the home, or from their peer group, these emotions can escalate to the point where they become strongholds. A stronghold is a loss of control on the part of the person because of the sins of the heart through a long indulgence to what is not right in God's sight. A stronghold might involve an eating disorder, anger within from a painful experience such as the death of a child, self-hatred, abuse of drugs and alcohol, aggression, or attacking others.

Ultimately, the emotions will spiral downward to depression and even thoughts of suicide if they are unaddressed. Many of the mass murder crimes in recent years have been committed by individuals who were consumed with deep-seated hurt and pain from rejection and abandonment.

How to Deal With Rejection and Abandonment
Recognize that you are a person of worth. You are wonderfully made by a God who loves you and sent His Son to die for you. If you had been the only person on earth, the sacrifice would not have been too much to make. God made you. He loves you. He desires for you to have restoration in your life. As a person of worth, you have true worth needs. Your true worth needs are:

Security. We all desire protection and security. This is an inherent need. If something in the home is out of control, it destroys our sense of protection and security. We are unable to be at ease or function normally and productively.

It isn't difficult to imagine the impact of lost security on people forced to leave their familiar places because of war and famine, or people in persecuted countries who fear the knock on the door they know is coming. We see terror in the eyes of children separated from their parents, and the hopelessness of parents desperate to provide security for their children.

In my years as a classroom teacher, I certainly saw the importance of security. I recognized very clearly that the majority of students want the classroom to be as orderly as possible. When it is, they feel secure and relaxed, and are able to work and learn. When one or two rascals are allowed to disrupt the classroom, the rest of the class feel disturbed and insecure.

Significance. Everyone needs to feel important and significant, and often, our significance is drawn from what we can or cannot do.

A teen who doesn't make the ball or soccer team may say to herself, "I'm not good enough to make the ball team, therefore I'm no good." In situations where one child in the family is favoured and esteemed above another, the less favoured may lack a sense of significance.

In my own youth, I would say, "Yeah, my name is Pringle, but who am I really?" I was a foster child, a welfare kid, totally unimportant. I believed I had no significance. Parents can make a big difference in building their children's significance.

Remember the poem earlier in the chapter?

> "Children deserve a little praise
> For tasks they're asked to do.
> If they're to lead a happy life,
> So much depends on you."

Acceptance. Everyone wants to be accepted as a person of worth regardless of his background. We want someone to pay attention to us, to say we are worthy of attention.

In my childhood, my need for acceptance was filled by Mrs. Ward, a teacher. It didn't matter to her that I wore big boots that left black marks on the floor. Mrs. Ward showed me love and acceptance, and I have never forgotten her.

Someone else who recognized this truth was Henry Hildebrand, the long-time president of Briercrest Bible Institute. Every Bible school student was required to prepare and deliver a sermon, and no matter how good or how pathetic it was, Hildebrand always made a point of praising the student for her effort. It didn't matter who they were, their background, or their giftedness; every student had equal worth in his eyes.

Many children who come from emotionally-damaged homes act out in hopes of being noticed and accepted. Others withdraw and develop despair-related conditions such as depression or anxiety. They get attention whatever way they can. If it's from good behaviour, that's fine, but if they don't get the attention they seek, they will also indulge in bad behaviour.

In the classroom, students who have trouble learning and know they are going to be asked a difficult question will often act out to try to divert attention from themselves and, hopefully, gain acceptance.

According to John 1:12, acceptance will always be found in Jesus: "But as many as received Him [Jesus], to them He gave the right to become children of God, to those who believe in His name."

Encouragement. Everyone thrives on being built up and encouraged. It gives us hope and confidence and the stimulation and impetus to develop the potential God has put within us.

Mark Twain observed, "Small people tend to belittle you but the really great make you feel that you, too, can become great." Even more encouraging is Jesus' promise that He will never leave us: "For lo, I am with you always, even to the end of the age" (Matthew 28: 20b). "Let your conduct be without covetousness; be content with such things as you have. For He Himself has said, 'I will never leave you nor forsake you'" (Hebrews 13:5). And: "Have I not commanded you? Be strong and of good courage; do not be afraid, nor be dismayed, for the Lord your God is with you wherever you go" (Joshua 1:9).

Discipline. Everyone needs it. It is essential in our lives. Without discipline, we can get ourselves in a lot of trouble.

The Bible has a lot to say about lack of discipline, sloth, and laziness (see Proverbs), but it also addresses the need for physical and spiritual discipline. In 1 Corinthians 9: 24-27, the Apostle Paul said, "Do you not know that those who run in a race all run, but one receives the prize? Run in such a way that you may obtain it. And everyone who competes for the prize is temperate in all things. Now they do it to obtain a perishable crown, but we for an imperishable crown. Therefore I run thus: not with uncertainty. Thus I fight, not as one who beats the air. But I discipline my body and bring it into subjection, lest when I have preached to others, I myself should become disqualified." Paul puts it another way in his advice to Timothy: "You therefore must endure hardship as a good soldier of Jesus Christ. No one engaged in warfare entangles himself with the affairs of this life, that he may please him who enlisted him as a soldier. And also if anyone competes in athletics, he is not crowned unless he competes according to the rules" (2 Timothy 2: 3–5).

Human beings function better within set parameters, but if the other true worth needs are not being met, discipline can lead to frustration, anger and bitterness which will keep us in bondage. The Bible teaches us to "Stand fast therefore in the liberty by which Christ has made us free, and do not be entangled again with a yoke of bondage" (Galatians 5:1).

Love. From God's perspective, love goes hand in hand with discipline. Hebrews 12: 6 says, "For whom the Lord loves He chastens [or disciplines]..." When we speak of love as a true worth need, we're talking about agape love, the kind of love that accepts people regardless of who they are, what they've done, or their background. This love comes only from God, who is the sixth true worth need.

God. Every human being has a need to worship something or Someone. We are created with an emptiness within that is only filled when Jesus Christ comes into our lives. That happens when we recognize and acknowledge that we have sinned, that there is nothing we can do in our own efforts to bridge the separation our sin has created between us and a Holy God. God had a plan. He sent his Son, Jesus Christ, to die in our place on the cross to make atonement for our sin. When that was accomplished, God raised Jesus from the dead and restored Him to His rightful place at God's right hand in Heaven.

The person who admits he has done wrong (sinned), sincerely asks forgiveness, and accepts the free gift of Christ's sacrifice in our place will not only be forgiven, but has access to a personal relationship with God and the promise of eternal life. That relationship with God provides healing from the emotional pain of rejection and abandonment.

If we flipped over the six true worth needs, we would see our individual worth from God's viewpoint.

- With God in our life, we have love. "For God so loved the world that He gave His only begotten Son, that whoever believes in Him should not perish but have everlasting life" (John 3:16).
- With God in our life, we have discipline. "I beseech you therefore, brethren, by the mercies of God, that you present your bodies a living sacrifice, holy, acceptable to God, which is your reasonable service" (Romans 12:1).
- Having God in one's life supplies encouragement. We are God's masterpiece. "For we are His workmanship, created in Christ Jesus for good works which God prepared beforehand that we should walk in them" (Ephesians 2:10).
- In God we know and experience acceptance. "My sheep hear My voice, and I know them, and they follow Me. And I give them eternal life, and they shall never perish; neither shall anyone snatch them out of My hand. My Father, who has given them to Me, is greater than all; and no one is able to snatch them out of My Father's hand. I and My Father are one" (John 10: 27-30).
- Knowing we belong to God gives us significance. John 10:29b assures us: "...No one is able to snatch them out of My Father's Hand."
- All of this gives security. "Yet in all these things we are more than conquerors through Him who loved us. For I am persuaded that neither death nor life, nor angels nor principalities nor powers, nor things present nor things to come, nor height nor depth, nor any other created thing, shall be able to separate us from the love of God which is in Christ Jesus our Lord" (Romans 8: 37-39).

God's Word and the person of the Lord Jesus Christ bring a person into a right relationship with God the Father, making him new in Christ. It also helps that person to reach out to others who have been hurt.

Practical steps for finding emotional healing

During my own spiritual journey to wholeness, I recognized that there were major steps to be taken in order to be emotionally free and whole. Most of this I learned through spending much time with God, because I was really a mixed-up, messed-up kid.

In later years, I have read other books that have been invaluable to solidify my own freedom and to recommend to clients. With individuals who I suspect have been involved with the occult and satanic experiences, I have them renounce any ungodly activity that will block their emotional healing.

Although I have put the following steps to finding emotional healing in an order, there are times I deal with more pressing needs than the order given. These practical steps are applicable for all emotional healing.

Step 1: Identify your wrong thoughts and feelings. Recognize the pain and the hurt. Call it what it is. I had to ask myself: "Why do I feel rejected and abandoned?" That was easy to figure out. My feelings of abandonment and rejection first occurred when my dad walked out of the home. They were reinforced when Mom let us be taken away. I felt like a piece of dirt. I felt rejected, unwanted, of no value to anyone—especially my parents. I told myself my mom must not love me, even though I knew she did. The truth was, she wasn't able to support and look after five kids. Naming the hurts helped them heal.

Step 2: Recognize that God is the only one who can heal the hurt. We like to try to fix things ourselves. We develop coping mechanisms like attacking others, running and hiding, getting into trouble at school or with the law, or in our sense of insignificance, trying to be recognized as somebody important and worthy of respect. But the Bible points to a more effective way: "For we do not have a High Priest who cannot sympathize with our weaknesses, but was in all points tempted as we are, yet without sin. Let us therefore come boldly to the throne of grace, that we may obtain mercy and find grace to help in time of need" (Hebrews 4: 15, 16). If we don't admit the hurt and pain, we cannot find healing.

Step 3: Choose to accept God's forgiveness. As individuals we need to realize, even though we are reacting out of pain that others have given to us, we have our own sin issues. The manner in which we respond to persons and situations has been pre-determined during the developmental stages of life. Acting out, fantasies, lying, stealing, aggressive and addictive behaviours are sinful and need to be confessed to God. God's Word gives us hope. "But if we confess our sins, He is faithful and just to forgive us our sins and to cleanse us from all unrighteousness" (1 John 1: 9). We must confess, and then God will forgive. Jesus Christ offers this rest from our burdens, but we must come in prayer to Him. "Come to Me, all you who labour and are heavy laden, and I will give you rest" (Matthew 11:28).

Step 4: Choose to forgive the people who have hurt you. Forgiveness is a deliberate choice. And it isn't easy, particularly if someone raped you three or four times a week for six years, or if your mom and dad abandoned you, or you've spent years being beaten up and no one stepped forward to protect you. It's not easy to forgive that. But genuine forgiveness has nothing to do with emotions. It has to do with your mind and your will. When forgiveness is a deliberate choice, the emotions will catch up over time. Forgiveness comes by saying, "God, I choose to forgive because that's what You require." In Matthew 6: 14, 15 Jesus says, "For if you forgive men their trespasses, your heavenly Father will also forgive you. But if you do not forgive men their trespasses, neither will your Father forgive your trespasses." I've had clients say to me, "I can't forgive." I say as gently as possible, "You really don't have any other choice. If you won't forgive, you can't be free."

I recall the wife of a lawyer who came to seek counseling because her husband was having an affair. She said, "I will never, ever forgive him." I said, "If you never forgive him, you will never heal from this. There is nothing I can do to help you. I cannot help you be free."

It is sad how many people in their senior years are still living with emotional pain and hurt because they have never forgiven what happened in their early life. They have robbed themselves of a life of fullness and richness.

Step 5: Choose to forgive yourself if you are part of the problem. How often we hear people lament, "I shouldn't have given in to my boyfriend." "I shouldn't have listened to him and had an abortion." "If only I hadn't agreed to drive the car my friend would not have been killed." They can't forgive themselves. When you have asked for God's forgiveness, you must choose to forgive yourself. You have to make a deliberate choice to say, "Because God has forgiven me, I choose to forgive myself," for whatever wrong you have done. People in my seminars often tell me this is the most powerful thing they've ever heard. I've had people say, "I've asked God a thousand times to forgive me, but I'm still stuck. After hearing what you've said, I see why."

We let ourselves out of prison by forgiving ourselves.

Step 6: Develop a daily spiritual walk that involves reading and studying the Bible, praying, and being obedient to the Lord. Only as you do that can you move forward to pull down the strongholds of rejection and abandonment. When working with new clients, I encourage them to begin reading the Bible in the book of Mark. It is fast-moving, and jumps right into the story of Jesus. Mark was written by a young man who was very close to Jesus. From there, it is easy to go on to the books of Luke and John, and then perhaps back to Matthew.

I also encourage the person to make a prayer list—a list of people and things for which they want to pray. I suggest they begin their prayer time with praise and worship using scripture like Psalm 100 or Psalm 103.

Step 7: Journaling. I often assign journaling homework to my clients. This is one of the most effective tools in achieving healing in any area of emotional illness. When they do their homework and journaling, the person is actively participating in achieving healing. Journaling involves deliberately spending time going back, identifying where the pain started, recalling specific hurtful events and experiences—and the people who hurt them—and writing it all down in the journal. Some clients hesitate at first because they have stuffed the painful memories very deep inside. They believe bringing them back to the surface will destroy what fragile hold they have on their emotions. Exactly the opposite is true.

I encourage clients to look at where their pain first started. Was their sense of rejection because of their parents' divorce? Perhaps the pain began when they first heard about divorce at the age of five or six. Up to that time, they'd felt pretty secure. Maybe things got worse and there were threats. Anger, bitterness, and even violence may have crept in. There was more pain when mom or dad finally walked out and the sense of rejection was overwhelming. Sometimes there was as much anger toward the one who stayed as the one who left.

I ask clients to describe their feelings when the events occurred, and as it went on. Over time, clients come to realize that there was rejection and pain all along the way. These individuals can identify feeling pain when their father missed their birthday or their mother missed their graduation or wedding. Journaling one's pain can be a profoundly healing process. I worked with a pastor who was having great difficulty, and was referred to me by a psychiatrist. I gave him a homework and journaling assignment. I asked him to spend a certain amount of time each day thinking about and writing down the instances in his life where he was hurt. He embraced the assignment aggressively, and the difference in him was noticeable immediately.

Barriers to Emotional Healing

My heart is grieved at times as some dear people I work with never receive emotional healing because of their own refusal to let go of their past and be free. Since I have prayed with many, many individuals and have seen God perform amazing miracles, I am sad when the response is no. Here are reasons why emotional healing cannot take place:

- Failure to accept God's love
- Failure to forgive others
- Failure to receive forgiveness
- Failure to forgive ourselves

- Failure to accept and love ourselves
- Failure to pull down strongholds of hurts and fears
- Failure to meet with God in a daily devotional time

Keys to freedom from rejection and abandonment

There are clearly definable keys to freedom from rejection and abandonment, that can open the door to a new life.

Key 1: Put your spiritual life in the right perspective. Be honest with God. Say, "God, is this where I failed You?" or "This is where people hurt me." Be specific. "Search me, O God, and know my heart; try me and know my anxieties, and see if there is any wicked way in me, and lead me in the way everlasting" (Psalm 139:23,24).

Key 2: Uncover other areas of hurts, failures, or places where Satan has attacked.

"For the Word of God is living and powerful, and sharper than any two-edged sword, piercing even to the division of soul and spirit, and of joints and marrow, and is a discerner of the thoughts and intents of the heart. And there is no creature hidden from His sight, but all things are naked and open to the eyes of Him to whom we must give account" (Hebrews 4:12, 13).

Key 3: Rest in Jesus Christ. He stated: "Come to Me, all you who labour and are heavy laden and I will give you rest" (Matthew 11:28).

Key 4: Stand strong in your freedom. Galatians 5:1 says, "Stand fast therefore in the liberty by which Christ has made us free, and do not be entangled again with a yoke of bondage."

How does one do this? In Christ's name, in Christ's blood, in Christ's Word, put on the armour of God and spend time in prayer. More will be given on this topic later.

Key 5: Uplift Christ through praise. "Bless the Lord, O my soul, and all that is within me, bless His holy name! Bless the Lord, O my soul, and forget not all His benefits: who forgives all your iniquities, who heals all your diseases, who crowns you with loving-kindness and tender mercies, who satisfies your mouth with good things so that your youth is renewed like the eagle's" (Psalm 103:1-5).

Key 6: Keep heaven and eternity as your key focus. Jesus states: "Let not your heart be troubled; you believe in God, believe also in Me. In My Father's house are many mansions; if it were not so, I would have told you. I go to prepare a place for you. And if I go and prepare a place for you, I will come again and receive you to Myself, that where I am, there you may be also" (John 14:1-3).

Counselors often ask themselves, when examining and dealing with very difficult situations: "How do we help those who have been destroyed emotionally by what they have been through? How can we reach out to them and see them set free?" The answer is that we must not reject the person they are, regardless of their background. They need to be encouraged to accept themselves as they are in the here and now. They need to understand the importance of having their temperament controlled by the Holy Spirit.

Praise and thanksgiving to God are also essential in the individual's emotional healing. Jesus Christ, the Great Physician, wants to set people free from their bad memories which include feelings, concepts, patterns, attitudes, and tendencies toward certain destructive actions.

It has been my privilege to pray with many people who have experienced rape, abortion, spousal abuse, child abuse, rejection, the occult, depression, fear, guilt, overbearing parents, and the like, and see God work in marvellous ways to set them free.

Before praying with clients for emotional healing, I ask them to share the difficult experiences they've gone through. In some cases, this involves homework prior to the session where the person has spent some time identifying and writing down or journaling their hurtful experiences. I ask them to describe the feelings that went along with each experience—feelings that are still recorded in the brain—and are a vital part of the recollection. I encourage them to think back to any other painful occurrences they may have forgotten, or put out of their mind.

In counseling, the following prayer procedure has shown itself to be effective again and again:

- The counselor binds the power of Satan over the client and renounces all authority of the Enemy over the individual. This is always done based on the authority of Jesus Christ, His shed blood, and the power of the Word of God.
- Always invite the Holy Spirit to be in control of the situation, to be the Comforter in this desperate time of need.
- Pray through the hurtful experiences the person has had, deliberately stopping at specific hurtful memories. There are times (as the counselor is open to the Holy Spirit's promptings) when other areas of trauma and hurt are brought to mind by the Holy Spirit. These traumatic experiences are also items for prayer. The counselor will invoke the healing power of the Lord Jesus Christ to minister healing in those specific areas.
- Following the prayer, the client is asked if there were any other areas that came to mind as we were praying. If there were, these areas of trauma are prayed for as well.
- If the client has been involved in the occult in any way, that needs to be renounced by the client in the name of the Lord Jesus Christ so that Satan can no longer have power over the person in that area.
- The client is encouraged to ask—through prayer—for forgiveness from God, as well as the ability to forgive others and to forgive themselves for what has been experienced.
- Rejoice together in the healing power of Christ.
- Follow-up sessions will be necessary to encourage and disciple the client.

Genuine healing can only come when the person is actively involved in the process. This means participating diligently in the homework and journaling. That, coupled with scripture, prayer, and choosing to forgive the one who hurt you, will break down any emotional stronghold. I guarantee it.

Prayer

"Lord, I have felt without hope, walking in a narrow, gloomy tunnel of rejection and abandonment. I cry out to You in my trouble; save me from my distress. Send forth Your Word; heal me and rescue me (Psalm 107:19, 20). You tell me in Your word that You are close to the broken-hearted and that you save those who are crushed in spirit (Psalm 34:18). I accept Your saving, healing and rescuing power in Jesus' name.

People have let me down; at times I've let myself down. This has happened so often I expect it without conscious thought. Forgive me for walking the walk of victims instead of marching the march of victors (1 John 5:4). "No, in all these things I am more than a conqueror through Jesus who loves me. For I am convinced that neither death nor life, nor angels nor demons, neither the present nor the future, nor any powers, neither height nor depth, nor anything else in all creation, will be able to separate me from the love of God that is in Christ Jesus my Lord" (Romans 8:37-39 NIV).

CHAPTER 3:
WHO DO YOU THINK YOU ARE?
THE DANGER OF LOW SELF-WORTH

This poignant letter was written by a small boy to a certain psycho-therapist, who hosts a mental health show called Ask the Doctor:

"Dear Doctor Garner:

What is bothering me is that long ago some big person, it is a boy about 13 years olde called me Turtle and I knew he said that because of my plastic sergery. And I think god hates me because of my lip. And when I die he will probably send me to hell. Love, Chris."

Chris had obviously drawn the conclusion that his disfigurement made him so worthless that not even God could love him. While that is completely illogical, many of us get bound up with emotions that have nothing to do with truth or logic. Young Chris felt that God hated him. He believed the same lie that is whispered in the ears of millions of people who are overwhelmed by inadequacy and inferiority.

"Who am I?" is a question everyone asks. The answer has nothing to do with name, position, ethnicity, or family background; it has everything to do with how people feel about themselves. It's about self-image—a term that is interchangeable with self-esteem, self-concept, self-worth and self-acceptance. If we are confident in ourselves, knowing we have done our best, we feel good about ourselves. We have accepted ourselves as people of worth. We have healthy self-image.

Unfortunately, too many are crippled by a poor sense of self-worth that, if not bolstered, can spiral them into deep depression and even suicide.

In our counseling ministry we have seen hundreds come out of that darkness and despair and walk in freedom. I am reminded of the words of David the psalmist in Psalm 40:2, 3 as he shares of God freeing him from the pit of despair. This is indeed the story of many that God has redeemed. "He also brought me up out of a horrible pit, Out of the miry clay. And set my feet upon a rock, And established my steps. He has put a new song in my mouth. Praise to our God; Many will see it and fear, And will trust in the Lord."

Suicide is officially the second most frequent cause of death among North Americans between the ages of 15 and 30. Suicide becomes the answer for far too many special people because these individuals cannot accept themselves. The deaths may be the result of abuse—physical, emotional, verbal or sexual. These desperate people perceive they have no self-worth, because of the mistreatment. How could one feel good about oneself when significant others have shown distain through mistreatment? It appears that one of the major problems plaguing children, young people, and adults today is a severe lack of self-acceptance.

Symptoms of low self-worth
What does low self-worth look like?

1. Perfectionism is a compulsion to have everything perfect and in order. Louise arrived at my office dejected and defeated with the presenting problem: "Help me. I'm nagging my children and I'm afraid I will destroy them." She stated that her children could never live up to her standards—rooms were not clean, beds were not made properly to her expectations. Louise hated herself because of her perfectionism. As I counseled her, I soon realized that Louise's mother had treated her the same way as a girl. Upon further investigation of the family, it was evident that Louise's grandmother was never satisfied with how her children performed. As Louise and I prayed about her painful past and her own sinful behaviour, God ministered to her and gave her children a cheerful, gentle, forgiving mother.

2. Wishful comparison with others affects every part of our society. Most individuals, if not all, are not totally satisfied with themselves or with their positions, whether it is the student, the athlete, the homemaker or the professional business woman or man. Myra was married to an influential medical doctor, but had struggled for years with accepting herself as a person of worth, and still was plagued by these feelings. On one occasion in counseling she mentioned that later that day, she was going out to buy a new dress for a special medical gala evening. Knowing that Myra had that tendency to compare herself with others, I asked who she dressed up for. She stated it was for her husband. I asked Myra if she also dressed up to impress other women. As Myra wrestled with my question, she admitted that it was true; her acceptance *was* based on how other women looked at her. Myra also said that most women compare themselves with other women and their self-worth is wrapped up in how they are received.

3. Excessive shyness or insecurity. Belinda, the only girl in the family with five boys, was teased unmercifully, to the point she was afraid to interact with other kids when she went to school. To make matters worse, her classmates picked up where her brothers left off. On most days at recess, she could be found gazing out the window at kids playing and refusing to take a chance to be a part of their games.

4. Feelings of inferiority. Living on the other side of the tracks can be more than a cliché. Sandra's family was extremely poor, having lost a husband, a loving father and the only breadwinner from cancer. Sandra's poor clothes and very skimpy lunch made her feel inferior to the other kids at school. Although she was not the one who caused the loss of her special Dad, Sandra was experiencing guilt and fear.

5. Inability to trust God. "I will never trust God again!" is a statement I have heard often in my counseling office. Stan had set his heart, in fact his whole life, on medicine. To be a doctor was what he believed God wanted for him. Low marks, and a negative review from the panel of supervisory doctors, forced Stan to look in other directions for a career. According to him, God had let him down. Stan felt he had done his part, but God did not follow through with His part.

6. Criticism of others. Often individuals criticize others because of their own issues of poor self-acceptance. Gerry seemed to make it his mission in life to be critical of others who had been successful in the business arena. Having failed in a number of business adventures, partly due to his own laziness, Gerry could often be heard in the local coffee shop condemning others who had made a name for themselves. Instead of gaining friends, people began to avoid him.

7. Unresolved personal problems. Ingrid was angry with herself for giving in to her boyfriend and was now the single parent of a baby girl. Ingrid had very few options for a job and her boyfriend was dating another young lady and refusing his parental responsibility. Ingrid was overwhelmed with her state of affairs. She ran herself down with extreme words of condemnation, and knew that her own behaviour was destroying her worth as a woman.

Individuals with poor self-image actually believe they have little worth. But beware! Thinking that way is a self-fulfilling prophecy. You become what you think. As Proverbs 23:7 says, "For as he thinks in his heart, so is he." So if you continually tell yourself, "I'm no good, and nobody likes me," you will soon discover that, in fact, nobody *does* like you. Who enjoys being with such a negative person?

Such a mindset often leads to escapism. Fantasy is a common avenue of escape from the harsh rejection of reality. The person lives in the never-never land of imagination, perhaps aided by television or novels. Another escape route that many choose is drugs and alcohol. The most desperate opt for the one-way route of suicide.

How is self-concept developed?

It is valuable to examine the factors that contribute to the development of a person's self-concept or how he views himself in relation to his world. Self-concept is learned. It is a complex and ongoing process that begins at birth and is influenced by the significant people in one's life. How we're treated by parents, teachers and peers all have an impact.

Sylvia's self-image was extremely low. She came from a poor, single-parent family. Because her mother was forced to work almost constantly, nine-year-old Sylvia had to fend for herself. She often came to school with messy hair and dirty, rumpled clothing. Her peers avoided her; teachers weren't always kind.

When Sylvia was brought to me for help, I began by counseling her mother. In this case, I believed that practical advice would help more than assigning scripture verses to read. I tried to impress upon Sylvia's mother the importance of her parenting job. We discussed the tremendous damage that had already been done and the necessity of making sure Sylvia was properly cared for. We explored together if there were practical ways that Sylvia's mother could make sure her daughter came first, even with her need to earn an income.

Sylvia had a lot of pain and hurt to work through. Part of it came from losing her other parent. It was interesting to me that as we successfully worked through Sylvia's issues, this young girl used the same methods to try to counsel her mother.

A person learns to view himself through successes and failures and from the reactions of others to his success. Unfortunately, what a person often views as truth is bound up in the world's idea of worth, which is based on The Four Ps: People: "It's who you know that counts." Prestige: "Reach for the top." Prosperity: "Money talks." Power: "Power comes from being in control."

In reality, people, prestige, prosperity, and power will not bring contentment or a truly healthy self-image. Legendary film star Judy Garland had every one of The Four Ps, yet reportedly attempted suicide twenty-one times before she finally succeeded.

When Dennis came to see me, he felt a complete failure and was deeply depressed. He had been involved in a large farming operation but sold out because of profound depression. Now he was afraid to use the capital from the farm sale to establish a business, because he'd tried other businesses and failed. Dennis had also tried Bible college, but quit that, too. Failure was a predictable part of his life, and his opinion of himself was as low as it could get.

Dennis's self-image was strongly influenced by his parents. His mother was sickly and fragile, while his father was a hard-driving man with high expectations. As a child, Dennis never seemed able to meet those expectations, something that helped shape his poor view of himself. If things he undertook were not perfect, Dennis quit. This led to guilt, self-hatred, fear, and ultimately deep depression.

Because of the profound hurts from childhood and his low self-image, Dennis was in serious need of emotional healing. Two books helped prepare him for this journey: *Inner Healing* by Betty Tapscott (Marshall, M&S, 1984) and *Do I Have To Be Me? Living With Yourself* by Lloyd Ahlem (Gospel Light Publications, 1981). As he read these books, Dennis became aware for the first time that God promises victory over fear, guilt and depression. God-given victory came about as I worked through a number of steps with Dennis. I prayed with him for emotional healing, and he was set free of the scars from his past. From the very first session onward, he showed progress in his walk with Christ, even though he continued to struggle with the belief that he had to win at any cost. From a life of fear, guilt and depression, Dennis was now experiencing God's power in his life. Jesus said in John 8:36, "Therefore if the Son makes you free, you shall be free indeed."

As Dennis became involved in systematic Bible study, memorization of scripture, and winning over Satan's attacks (by praying to bind and renounce the evil power), he found the freedom he longed for. His business enterprises began to flourish and he was blessed financially. His marriage, which had been seriously strained, also gained new levels of love and happiness.

A person's early self-concept, developed by parents and siblings, plays a large role. If parents have shared positive and encouraging statements with their child, the impact will be positive. The opposite is also true. Mistreatment, belittlement, and criticism produce a sense of worthlessness.

Allan was a young man who came from a wealthy family in a farming community. Allan got along well with other people, but at home, his father refused to allow him to drive the tractor or be involved in any of the important aspects of farm life. All of this gave Allan the impression that he was incapable, that he couldn't do anything right. The spin-offs from this were dire. Allan's marriage faltered and due to his poor self-image he was unable to hold a job for any length of time.

And then there was Sherry, whose mother was a perfectionist. Sherry said to me, "Even now that I'm an adult, my mother continually complains about how I look, what I wear, how I speak, how I raise my children." I suspect that Sherry's mother was deeply insecure herself, and by imposing unrealistic expectations on her daughter and grandchildren, she only perpetuated the damage.

Parents have a profound impact on how a child's sense of self develops. A common wrong is giving children the impression that if they don't meet certain expectations they are not accepted or approved. Whether spoken aloud or not, the message is abundantly clear: "You are only worthy if you measure up to this standard."

Parents in this category need to deal with their own fears, insecurities, and guilt, and their perfectionism and sense of failure. They must determine, by God's grace, not to perpetuate their own shortcomings in their children.

Parents, if you have done this, you need to confess it to God and to your child. Say, "I am going to leave that behind. I will love and accept my child just as God the Father accepts me in Christ."

Read this parent's prayer (author unknown) over carefully, and consider making it a part of your prayer life, if you are a parent.

A Parent's Prayer

"Heavenly Father, make me a better parent. Teach me to understand my children, to listen patiently to what they have to say, and to answer all their questions kindly. Keep me from interrupting them or contradicting them. Make me as courteous to them as I would have them be to me. Forbid that I should ever laugh at their mistakes, or resort to shame or ridicule when they displease me. May I never punish them for my own selfish satisfaction or to show my power. Let me not tempt my child to lie or steal. And guide me hour by hour that I may demonstrate by all I say and do that honesty produces happiness. Reduce, I pray, the meanness in me. And when I am out of sorts, help me, O Lord, to hold my tongue. May I ever be mindful that my children are children, and I should not expect them to have the judgement of adults. Let me not rob them of the opportunity to wait on themselves and make decisions. Bless me with the bigness to grant them all their reasonable requests and the courage to deny them privileges I

know will do them harm. Make me fair and just and kind, and fit me, O Lord, to be loved and respected and imitated by my children."

My self-worth as a child was extremely low, and because of that, I frequently acted out. I have recollections of being in grade one in a one-room school and already having a low sense of worth. I recall an incident when an older child was going to beat up my sister. I ran to protect her and the big kid started beating on me. The teacher threatened to strap me, and when I headed for the door, she sent the big guy to stop me. I felt completely, utterly helpless, and worthless. It didn't help my self-image to go home that day and find my mom sleeping with her boyfriend. I wanted my mother to console me, to listen to my side of the story, to tell me everything would be fine, but she was preoccupied with a man who I despised.

School is the second most important influence in building a child's self-concept. How you feel about yourself during the school years is centered in whether you do well and are accepted, or whether you struggle and are bullied and picked on. Jonathan longed to be on the soccer team, even though he was small and not well-coordinated. He tried out, but didn't make it. He felt worthless, a failure. For months afterward, soccer team members teased him, calling him "Runt," "Puny," and "Girlie." This made him feel even more useless and unworthy. He became angry and depressed.

When Jonathan came for help, I knew it was essential to have him channel his focus in another direction. Even as a fourteen-year-old, Jonathan needed to recognize that he had gifts and talents other than playing soccer. Like so many people, he was fixated on his shortcomings. I advised Jonathan's parents to encourage and built him up in those areas where they knew he had competence.

Jonathan also learned the tool of avoiding verbal attacks, and when he did encounter one, to rebuke it in the name of Jesus and refuse to accept the statement.

Sadly, damage during the school-age years is sometimes done by a teacher. During counseling, Georgia related how in her early years in school she often had to do work on the blackboard. Being shy, fearful, and insecure, she invariably made mistakes. The teacher made matters worse by criticizing and humiliating Georgia in front of her peers, and encouraging the rest of the class to laugh at her.

It is important to note that low self-esteem or a poor self-concept is not exclusive to the slow learner. Everyone—learning disabled, under-achiever, over-achiever, and even the gifted child—can struggle with self-image.

Jenny, for instance, was a student in my high school English class who gave the appearance of being cheerful and in good spirits most of the time. She was involved in the sports program and seemed to cope well with the dynamics of school. Some years later, however, she came to my counseling office a broken, despairing young woman. Jenny had tried to commit suicide multiple times because it seemed she was incapable of making her grades at university. She felt a complete failure and believed the best thing to do was kill herself.

Part of Jenny's sense of inadequacy was rooted in pressure from her father, a physician with high aspirations for his children. The expectation to excel was more than Jenny could handle. Her struggle with low self-esteem and trying and failing to meet her father's expectations was a continual battle that she just wanted to end.

Jenny was able to win the struggle by developing a personal daily Bible study time and memorizing scripture that helped her look at herself from God's perspective. One verse that helped her tremendously was Ephesians 2:10 which says, "For we are His workmanship, created in Christ Jesus for good works, which God prepared beforehand that we should walk in them."

Why can't I accept myself?

Fear, guilt, failures, bitterness, anger, lack of love and insecurity all give rise to an inability to accept oneself.

In my practice, when I'm dealing with a client in the area of self-acceptance, I will ask the person to fill out the following questionnaire, *The Positives and Negatives In My Life*, by completing each sentence. This is particularly helpful for young people who sometimes have a hard time verbalizing what they're feeling. If you would like to understand your innermost feelings in this area, complete the sentences yourself. Try to be honest about how you really feel:

1. My happiest time.....................
2. Some people........
3. I like...............................
4. I would like to know.................
5. My greatest fear......................
6. What worries me........................
7. What bothers me........................
8. My nerves............................
9. I.....................................
10. I need.............................
11. The future............................
12. I feel..........
13. I regret.......................
14. I desire........................
15. I am extremely...................
16. I can't.........................
17. What hurts me....................
18. I secretly......................
19. I failed.........................
20. I dislike........................

One young man answered statement number five by writing: "My greatest fear is 11:34." When I questioned his answer, he told me 11:34 on a digital clock is hell spelled backwards, and that's what he saw when he woke up every night at 11:34. He dreaded waking up. We prayed specifically about that and God delivered the young man from his fear of 11:34. He no longer woke up at 11:34, but sleeps right through the night.

Please also fill out the questionnaire below which will enable you to delve deeper into the heart of your self-perception.

1. Do I know my purpose for living? Yes No
2. Do I like/love myself? Yes No
3. Are friends and neighbours a threat to me? Yes No
4. Would I call myself a self-disciplined person? Yes No
5. Do I feel loved by my family? Yes No
6. Do I have a willingness to accept others with love and understanding? Yes No

7. If I had a choice to change myself, would I? Yes No
8. Do I feel free to be myself or do I have to pretend or put on a front? Yes No
9. Do I feel that I need to be constantly producing in order to be accepted? Yes No
10. Can I put my finger on what is missing in my life? Yes No

Sometimes poor self-image is hidden, as is revealed in the following poem by Edwin Arlington Robinson. Written in 1837, it describes a man who struggled with a negative sense of self, despite seemingly having it all.

Richard Cory

Whenever Richard Cory went downtown,
We people on the pavement looked at him:
He was a gentleman from sole to crown,
Clean-favoured and imperially slim.
And he was always quietly arrayed,
And he was always human when he talked
But still he fluttered pulses when he said,
"Good morning," and he glittered when he walked.
And he was rich—yes, richer than a king—
And admirably schooled in every grace:
In fine, we thought that he was everything
To make us wish that we were in his place.
So on we worked, and waited for the light
And went without the meat, and cursed the bread;
And Richard Cory, one calm summer night,
Went home and put a bullet through his head.

It is often the conflict between our ideal self and our real self that precipitates problems of self-acceptance. There is the real me and the person I would like to be, and the further the ideal me is from the real me, the worse it is for the person's sense of self-worth.

In Lloyd Ahlem's book *Do I Have To Be Me?* the author offers several avenues of false thinking that may contribute to the disparity between the real me and the ideal me, the one I dream I can be:
- If you never admit something bothers you, it won't.
- If you put a lid on troubled feelings.
- If you deny difficult emotional experiences.
- If you protect your image at any cost.

Ahlem writes that people with a low self-worth are the product of individuals, communities, congregations, or families who respect people only if they turn out "right" according to predetermined stereotypes. If your life is suspect, they consider you inferior.

How to Find a Christian Therapist

- First of all, realize that seeking counseling is an excellent first step to spiritual healing. Many, many Christians benefit from having a safe place where they can share anything and everything in confidence.
- Many pastors or ministers will recommend trained, licensed and trusted therapists in or near your community. Ask your pastor for a recommendation.
- Google "Christian counselors" to find an office near you. Many counseling offices have websites that list the professional credentials and areas of speciality of their counselors.

How to build an adequate self-worth

Psychologists say there are three basic needs in every individual: a need to be loved, a need to belong, and a need to contribute to society.

I would add a fourth basic need, one that I believe is more important than all the others. Every person has a need to know God in a personal way through Jesus Christ. Where love is conditional, where acceptance is dependent on one's performance, and where one's attempts at contributing to society or to the family unit are depreciated or seen as inadequate, a low self-esteem results. God the Father's acceptance of those who put their faith in Jesus Christ is unconditional. It is based on Jesus Christ's perfect life and upon His sacrifice when He died at Calvary. Accepting Jesus into your life meets the fourth need, and helps in the other three areas as well, since life with Christ has new meaning and direction.

The first step in building a healthy self-image is recognizing that—in God's eyes—you are loved.

If you have a low opinion of yourself, reconsider. **You are worthwhile.** You were created by God, for God's honour and glory. God has expressed Himself in you as Genesis 1:26, 27 states: "we are made in God's image after His likeness." Wow! If you despise yourself, you are discrediting your Creator. "For we are His workmanship, created in Christ Jesus for good works, which God prepared beforehand that we should walk in them" (Ephesians 2:10).

You are honoured by God. "Behold what manner of love the Father has bestowed on us, that we should be called children of God! Therefore the world does not know us, because it did not know Him. Beloved, now we are children of God; and it has not yet been revealed what we shall be, but we know that when He is revealed, we shall be like Him, for we shall see Him as He is" (1 John 3:1-2).

You are valued and loved by God. "But God demonstrates His own love toward us, in that while we were still sinners, Christ died for us" (Romans 5:8).

You are chosen by God. He has carefully planned for you. "... just as He chose us in Him before the foundation of the world, that we should be holy and without blame before Him in love, having predestined us to adoption as sons by Jesus Christ to Himself, according to the good pleasure of His will" (Ephesians 1: 4-5).

You have been forgiven by God. Once we receive Jesus Christ into our life, the Father looks at us as if we had never sinned. Jesus died to forgive our sins. Without Jesus in your life, you are nowhere near what you could be. It is Christ's righteousness only that makes us acceptable to God. Paul in Titus 3:4-7 writes: "But when the kindness and the love of God our Savior toward man appeared, not by works of righteousness which we have done, but according to His mercy He saved us, through the washing of regeneration and renewing of the Holy Spirit, whom He poured out on us abundantly through Jesus Christ our Savior, that having been justified by His grace we should become heirs according to the hope of eternal life."

My own self-esteem did not come together until I made a deliberate commitment of my life to Jesus Christ. Ephesians 2:8-10 convinced me I needed to do this. It says, "For by grace you have been saved through faith, and that not of yourselves; it is a gift of God, not of works, lest anyone should boast. For we are His workmanship, created in Christ Jesus for good works, which God prepared beforehand that we should walk in them."

I realized that only God's grace could save me from my life the way it currently was. I acknowledged that I was a sinner; I believed that Jesus Christ died to pay for my sins, and I confessed my sin to Him. Out of that came the sense that I could accept myself because of God's grace and forgiveness in my life. Prior to that, any good feelings I had about myself had come when I excelled in sports, or played in the dance band, or had a pretty girl on my arm. None of those good feelings lasted. I realized that no matter how good our band was, there would always be other singers, other musicians, other guitar players that would be better. You will always bump into someone who is bigger, stronger, prettier, or more talented.

When I started to understand and accept that I was God's workmanship, His masterpiece (See Ephesians 2:8-10), I realized I didn't have to follow any criteria—my own or anyone else's—to be acceptable. God already accepts me even with all my struggles and fears, because He loves me.

Gene had one of the worst self-images of anyone I ever counseled. He was timid, introverted, fearful, lonely and depressed. Although he was a Christian, Gene could not get rid of constant emptiness and frustration. He also felt extremely guilty because he couldn't rid himself of a two-pack-a-day cigarette habit. He believed if he could be delivered from that, his depression would leave and he would see himself as a more adequate person. When he was a new Christian and wanted to be baptized, one of the church leaders who opposed the baptism on the grounds of Gene's smoking habit walked out during the ceremony. Gene was crushed. He felt even more worthless.

Before Gene could find release from the cigarettes, he needed to realize that his self-esteem had to be healed through the power of Jesus Christ as he surrendered to Him (John 8:36). I gave him *Do I Have To Be Me?* to read. We discussed it, along with Bible passages from Romans 8 and Psalm 139 which expound on the intricacies of human birth, God's love and kindness, and His kind and watchful eye over us at all times.

Kenneth Taylor's paraphrase of Psalm 139: 13-18 in *The Living Bible* expresses it beautifully: "You made all the delicate, inner parts of my body, and knit them together in my mother's womb. Thank you for making me so wonderfully complex! It is amazing to think about. Your workmanship is marvellous—and how well I know it. You were there while I was being formed in utter seclusion! You saw me before I was born and scheduled each day of my life before I began to breathe. Every day was recorded in your Book. How precious it is, Lord, to realize that you are thinking about me constantly! I can't even count how many times a day your thoughts turn toward me. And when I waken in the morning, you are still thinking of me!"

Gene was faithful in reading the assigned books, studying and memorizing scripture, and in witnessing for Christ. Finally, on a pre-arranged day, we prayed a prayer for his release from his cigarette habit. Gene has not smoked a cigarette since.

As he remained faithful in his relationship with Christ, God met Gene's other needs, too. A lovely Christian woman came into his life. They both came to me for pre-marital counseling, and today are happily married.

Many people are angry at God for the way He made them. They feel inferior because of their physical appearance. Gene's issues did not stem from his physical appearance, but for many people their body image is a huge issue. The girl who wants to be smaller, the young man who wants to be strong and muscular, so he can make the football team and even the overweight pastor who wants to look good in front of his congregation. I encourage clients to look at the inside, and recognize that God has made them beautiful.

Accepting Jesus Christ as one's personal Saviour and Lord is the foundation upon which a positive self-acceptance is built. Christianity is not a religion; it is a relationship. Here are some steps to work on that relationship:

- Begin a relationship with God the Father through His Son Jesus Christ. Jesus said, "Come to Me, all you who labour and are heavy laden, and I will give you rest" (Matthew 11:28). Jesus offers to take your load of problems, insecurities, anxieties, and inferiorities.

- Accept His forgiveness. "If we confess our sins, He is faithful and just to forgive us our sins and to cleanse us from all unrighteousness" (1 John 1:9). Believe this. Accept it, because it means you!

- Forgive yourself; accept yourself. By an act of the will say, "God, You forgave me, so I forgive myself." Please read Romans 8:31–39 to see God's love for you.

- Forgive others who have hurt you, humiliated you, and put you down. That parent or teacher who criticized you or embarrassed you must be forgiven; otherwise you will never be able to fully accept yourself. Free yourself of the resentment and animosity that has gnawed at your soul for years and poisoned your interpersonal relationships. If you have been deeply hurt through physical, emotional or sexual abuse, you may need to see a Christian counselor or a pastor who understands abuse. Healing and forgiveness in these areas take longer to accomplish, but do not give up. Keep working at it.

- Desire to walk in the Holy Spirit. Pray, "God I don't want sin in my life. I want to live in Your power and strength." The Holy Spirit will enable you to do so.

- Identify wrong thoughts, feelings and actions. Identify the negativism in your life and change your negative way of thinking. If you feel inferior, if you think you are of little worth, if you are fearful and insecure, you will act this out by withdrawal and by various degrees of self-destruction. Get out of the vicious cycle of negative thinking and casting blame. Don't say, "It's my parents' fault I'm in this predicament." Set your mind on Jesus

Christ. Think on positive things. Read your Bible and pray and "the peace of God which surpasses all understanding will guard your hearts and minds through Christ Jesus" (Philippians 4:7).

Many Christians do not accept themselves because they have an ambivalent relationship with God. I have heard believers say, "I know God's Word states that He loves me, but because of my past, I honestly don't feel that He forgives and accepts me." What they're really saying is: "I can't forgive myself for my past, and consequently, I have difficulty accepting myself."

Lori was a single woman who felt inferior to others for as long as she could remember. Consequently, people—especially men—took advantage of her. She had been raped several times. She had difficulty believing that Jesus could really love her.

A number of areas had to be dealt with in order to free Lori. She resented her father for making her mother into a depressed and fearful woman, and since Lori had such a poor father image, she believed the same was true of God. Given the rapes, she had a hard time trusting any man.

Lori had serious problems with anxiety, depression, inhibition, sub-jectivity and hostility. We used the Bible to start a program to alleviate these stress factors. Since Lori didn't have a consistent Bible study and devotional plan of her own, I gave her one, and encouraged her to read one chapter of the Bible every day. She was to write a summary of the chapter, the key verse, and the lessons she learned from the day's reading. On an appointed day, we also prayed for emotional healing from the bad childhood experiences and the sexual abuse.

Lori had difficulty letting go and allowing Jesus Christ to control all the areas of her life, but over time, she made progress. Following the prayer for emotional healing, she was able to meet with God in a more consistent way, and instead of viewing God as always being out to punish her, she came to accept God's love and forgiveness, and ulti-mately, to forgive herself.

Gradually Lori's self esteem became positive, her job less of a burden, and she was established in a Gospel-preaching church. As she gained a sense of inner calmness and security, she was able to be more open with

Christian men and eventually married a fine Christian husband. Today, Lori is a pastor's wife.

God accepts us unconditionally on the merits of Jesus Christ alone. Titus 3:5, 6 teaches that it is "...not by works of righteousness which we have done, but according to His mercy He saved us, through the washing of regeneration and renewing of the Holy Spirit, whom He poured out on us abundantly through Jesus Christ our Saviour." Ephesians 2:8, 9 says it this way: "For by grace you have been saved through faith, and that not of yourselves; it is the gift of God, not of works, lest anyone should boast." Because of Christ's death, His resurrection, and His coming again, we have the right to accept ourselves.

An excellent tool to remove stress from our lives is to realize that when we are followers of Christ, God sees Jesus when He looks at us. That makes all the difference in the world.

Beware the Self-life
The self-life is in direct opposition to God. It comes from the Enemy of our souls and is characterized by living for and relying on one's own self.

Characteristics of the self-life include:

Self-reliance: "I don't need God. I am my own god and master of my own fate."

Self-centeredness: The Me, Me, Me Syndrome. It is narcissistic and almost childish in mentality, and screams, "That's my toy" or "Meet my need."

Self-indulgence: The "Eat, drink and be merry" philosophy.

Self-seeking: "Look at me. See how great I am?" This is often considered the actor/rock star mentality, but we sometimes see it even in our church pulpits.

Self-pity: Feeling sorry for oneself and focusing exclusively on one's own problems and woes. If not dealt with, it can lead to suicide.

Self-loathing: "I hate myself so much I want to die" and "I'm so fat, I hate myself." This destructive attitude leads to eating disorders, slashing, cutting, and the use of illicit drugs.

In the Bible, Galatians 5:1 commands us to: "Stand fast therefore in the liberty by which Christ has made us free, and do not be entangled again with a yoke of bondage." We will avoid being further "entangled in a yoke of bondage" if we steer clear of the self-life.

The Lies Satan Tells

We must also be aware of the lies Satan loves to tell us:

"You are the master of your own destiny."

"There is no heaven and no hell; when you die you no longer exist. Therefore, you can sin and get away with it."

"There are no absolutes, no moral standards. Do whatever you want."

"There is no one true God."

"How can you really know God?"

"Jesus isn't God."

"You can always be saved tomorrow."

"There are many ways to get to heaven."

"Satan is more powerful than God. If God is so powerful, how come bad things happen?"

Reject such lies and remember that our real self-worth is in God. When we seek Him, and put Him first in our life, He will give us the strength and grace to live the abundant life regardless of our circumstances. I am completely amazed when I read of accounts of suffering, persecuted believers who continue to praise their Savior Jesus Christ in spite of the cruelest torture imaginable.

How do we test what we are hearing?

- Share your thoughts with a trusted Christian friend.
- Read scripture to determine if your thoughts match with God's Word.
- Establish a daily time of prayer and Bible reading, even if you begin with five minutes a day.
- Write a favourite passage on a small card and carry it with you. When you begin to think unhealthy thoughts that might be coming from the Enemy, take out that card and read your verse.

Feelings of inferiority and the resulting insecurity come from a person's perceived inability to measure up to expectations. These expectations may be put on the individual by parents, teachers, peers, or even the people themselves. High expectations, without the means of measuring up to them, can be devastating.

God also has a set of high standards for us. In fact, His standard is nothing less than perfection. But He has provided a means of meeting that standard. He gave His only Son, Jesus Christ, who is perfect, to die in our place to make payment for our sins and wrongdoing. When we accept the gift of Christ's sacrifice, we are received by God the Father as perfect and as sinless as Jesus Himself.

This poem, written by Dr. C. R. Solomon, a Christian psychologist and author of *Handbook to Happiness*, speaks to a fundamental human need, that of acceptance.

> ...Being valued by others I love
> Enhances my own feeling of worth.
> Oh, the release and freedom He gives
> As I behold His wonderful face—
> As Jesus makes real my acceptance in Him,
> And I learn the true meaning of grace.

As I conclude the chapter, this prayer contains similar statements that I have heard in counseling sessions over the years.

"Dear Heavenly Father:

Why is it that I am never satisfied with who I am? Daily I wrestle with fears and inadequacies based not on how You see me, but on how I see myself or sense others see me. I am so disappointed when I resent others for their successes, power and position.

Inwardly I complain that my experience in life and even my walk with You Lord is so mundane and uneventful. I want the joy of the Lord to be my strength and fulfillment, but my self-centered thoughts keep me from being the person You created me to be. Jesus, You say in Your Word, "Come to Me when you are weak and burdened down and I will give you rest." That is my desire Lord, but my own insecurity screams at me as my accuser, "You are always coming to Jesus with the same list of complaints, but you never receive His victory; He must be getting tired of you!"

Father, I want the victory You have promised to me. I desire to shed the grave clothes of my lack of trust, self centeredness and destructive self-talk. I choose, Lord Jesus, to come boldly to Your throne of grace and receive Your love, Your power, Your acceptance, Your cleansing and Your freedom that You promised to me. Thank you Father that today will be the beginning of a full and meaningful life. Amen"

CHAPTER 4: EXPECTING THE WORST: STRESS, WORRY AND FEAR

Barry is a 48-year-old businessman who pushes himself unmercifully. He came from a home where there was alcohol abuse, constant fighting, criticism and financial disasters. That, coupled with the fact that he was told as a young man that he wouldn't amount to anything, pushes him to strive for ever-increased success in his career. He knows his desperation to succeed is an attempt to fulfill a need in his own life created by his father's contention that Barry was useless. Barry's marriage is suffering, and so is his relationship with his children. He smokes heavily, goes on occasional drinking binges, and has ongoing periods of heat flashes and chest pains. At times Barry is afraid to go to bed at night, fearful that he won't wake up in the morning.

Bonnie—52, married, and a school teacher—came from a very legalistic religious family with little love or security. All her life she has felt she would only be accepted and worthwhile if she performed consistently at the optimum level.

Her situation at school is growing intolerable. Sometimes even a minor misdemeanour on the part of a student can create such overwhelming fits of anger that Bonnie knows she must either get help or quit teaching. Deep down, she knows it isn't just the children she is having trouble with, it's her own past. Anger and bitterness against her home, her parents, and extended family are a constant source of pain.

Bonnie's medical doctor has suggested she receive counseling in order to deal with her stress, but there are times she thinks suicide is the only real solution.

The tragic stories of Barrie and Bonnie are all too familiar. In our society these sad sagas are repeated over and over again. It is obvious that people are calling for help as they verbally state: "I am so stressed out!" "The stress is killing me!" and "I don't know if I can live under this pressure much longer." These are familiar phrases to those who live in a hectic world. For most of us, the hectic world is our normal sphere, even though we know stress can be emotionally, physiologically, mentally and spiritually dangerous.

Too much stress ultimately exhausts the body's ability to adapt. Vital organs wear out and various illnesses can appear. This is especially true when stress is perceived to be negative or harmful.

Some of the complaints or symptoms that I've heard in counseling stressed people are: difficulty sleeping; agitated emotions; inability to concentrate; headaches that are long lasting; very little appetite; libido and digestive problems. People experience irritability, fear of heart attack because of chest pains, rapid breathing, ulcers and other undiagnosed body complaints.

Of course, there is also stress that helps us perform at our best. We call this optimal stress. The body can tolerate this kind of stress and, in fact, it provides the motivation needed to accomplish what needs to be done. Another kind of stress is eustress. This is stress that is generated in response to any happy event or occurrence that is in some way demanding—like a graduation, a marriage, or even a vacation. Distress is the kind of stress we all fear. Distress involves those things that cause negative emotions like sadness, anger, fear, or anxiety.

Hans Selye, the Canadian doctor who first introduced stress to the world as a scientific concept back in 1936, outlined the Stress Response in a three-stage process:

1. Alarm Stage (Fight-or-Flight Response): the body is activated by a stressor; the coping mechanisms of the mind and body prepare for operation. These responses are both physiological and psychological. The fight-or-flight response pumps powerful stress hormones and steroids into the blood stream. (It is important to understand that these responses are to acute stress, not chronic stress. Acute stress is passing; serious damage to the body results from the fight-or-flight response to chronic stress.)

2. Resistance Stage: the body is a magnificent instrument, and in this stage, the response to the stressor is channelled to a specific organ system. This adaptation process can contribute to chronic illness. If stress continues over a long period of time, the organ system may become exhausted and start to malfunction. Headaches, forgetfulness, colon spasms, anxiety attacks, and high blood pressure may result.

3. Exhaustion Stage: the organ system that dealt with the Resistance Stage breaks down. Disease, malfunction of the organ system, or death can occur. Cardiovascular disease, as well as high blood pressure-related maladies, has been closely linked to stress and its repercussions.

Dr. Norman Wright, in his book *The Pillars of Marriage* (95-96, used by permission) offers ten potential causes of stress. Take a moment to ask yourself if any of these affect you right now. If they do, what can be done about them?

1. An unresolved relationship
If you have uncertainties about your marriage (wondering if your partner is unhappy or thinking of leaving you) stress is present. This kind of burden can colour your attitude toward all areas of life.

2. Your environment
A monotonous and repetitious environment can contribute to stress and be as much a problem as a fast-paced, pressure-filled, competitive atmosphere.

3. Perfectionism
Having excessively high standards sets you up for failure and self-rejection. A perfectionist spouse is hard to live with because no one is or can be perfect. The only perfect and sinless person to live on earth was Jesus

Christ. Perfectionism generates insecurity. Secure people are flexible and willing to take risks and make positive changes, but when we have unrealistic expectations and don't live up to them, we begin to despise ourselves—something that can lead to depression.

4. Impatience
If you are impatient with others, you are probably impatient with yourself, as well. Not getting things done according to your schedule can keep your insides in turmoil.

5. Rigidity
Rigidity is a continual state or attitude of being inflexible. We may be amused at this statement, "My way or the highway," but that arrogance is self-serving and destructive, rather than being healthy or helpful. This is closely tied to perfectionism and impatience. Rigid people spend their time prospecting for something to be upset about.

6. Inability to Relax
Can you sit in a chair for ten minutes and totally relax? Or does your mind keep running over everything you need to do? Do you constantly push yourself at a hurried pace?

7. Explosiveness and Anger
If your life is characterized by bombs spreading angry shrapnel at others, stress is not only affecting you, it's affecting the people you care about. Expressing anger is better than bottling it up, but continual outbursts do not help anyone, including you.

8. Lack of Humour and Little Enthusiasm
People who are filled with self-conceit, self-reproach, (and therefore, stress) are probably depressed, as well.

9. Too Much Competition
Comparing ourselves with others in terms of what they do and what they have puts unneeded pressure on us. Why should what others do and say have an affect on our state of mind? Some competition in certain

areas can be fun and enjoyable, but when competition is constant, it is no longer fun.

10. Lack of Self-worth

Low self-esteem is the basis for many of our difficulties, and it can involve stress and depression. If you feel you lack importance or influence in your marriage or family dynamics, it may be because you see yourself as being of little value, you have tacitly encouraged your spouse or other family members to treat you in such a way that your feeling is reinforced.

In my practice I have witnessed client after client exhibiting the signs of stress. Christians are not exempt from this condition, nor the negative health results that grow from it if left unchecked.

Dr. Marion H. Nelson, a Texas psychiatrist, who wrote *Why Christians Crack Up* (Moody Press, 1974. Used by permission), shared insights on spiritual causes of stress and psychological disorders. Read Nelson's categories and see if they fit you or someone you love:

1. The failure to recognize God as a Person who is capable of loving and is interested in us as His creation.
2. Lack of respect for our own bodies.
3. Resisting God's regulating laws for our lives.
4. Failure to yield to the proper authority of God.
5. Sin in our life.
6. Failure to obey, or lack of proper development of a conscience.
7. Physical and emotional weakness of people.
8. The effect of the world on Christians.
9. Failure to arrange priorities, time, and commitments correctly.
10. Covetousness.
11. Tendency to avoid reality and responsibility. We know as believers in Christ, we have been given accountability to be good stewards of His resources. There are times that we neglect His directives and grieve His Holy Spirit.
12. Satanic attack. In Revelation 12 we are told that Satan is the accuser of believers. He does that through fear, lies and creating doubt in our minds.

Having these insights on stress is actually good news for the Christian. If we know that there are spiritual causes for stress, then there must be spiritual solutions as well. From my own experience of counseling professional people such as teachers, pastors, doctors and lawyers—professions with high stress levels—I have used this list of conditions that can create stress in an individual:

1. **What are my expectations?** Unrealistic idealism only creates problems for an individual. Take Joseph for instance who wants to become a medical doctor, but his grade point average prevents him from that ultimate goal.
2. **Pressures of the workplace affect one's family relationships.** This would include being controlled by our co-workers. Bryce, through counseling, is beginning to realize that his anger towards his family results from destructive relationships at work and things must change.
3. **Achievement, regardless of the cost!** The desire to continually produce in a performance game in which we become trapped can create great stress.
4. **The belief that we need to be all things to all people,** which is impossible and will lead to burnout.
5. **Perfectionism** - the frustration of the professional's spouse who has to be perfect because of the person to whom they are married.
6. **Pressures** and stress can create very serious marital problems.
7. **Children** who cause parents grief and trouble put severe pressure and stress upon them.
8. **Working with individuals who have severe problems** (medical, emotional, mental, and marital, etc.) can cause one extreme stress. Over the years, I have counseled others in the helping professions, such as pastors who state they are burned out because of the constant stress of working with needy people.

Although the causes and manifestations of stress might differ from person to person, I have discovered that the help I was able to offer as a counselor tended to remain fairly constant.

Counseling Helps for the Stressed

1. Accept the fact that stress is inevitable and that not all stress is bad.
2. Recognize the early warnings signs of burnout. It is important to listen to significant others, such as family members, when they are concerned for us.
3. Develop an active support system. I know of men who meet weekly in an accountability group as a support for each other.
4. Come to grips with the problem as early as possible. Far too many people ignore the obvious signs to their own detriment.
5. Practice stress transfer and thereby break the stress pattern. For example, move it from the emotional to the physical by becoming physically active. Find physical things to do in and around the house. Refuse to sit and allow wrong thoughts to control you.
6. Get plenty of physical exercise.
7. Take sufficient time off work. We may applaud the one who states, "I'm a workaholic," but we are all aware of the consequences of that mentality.
8. Organize your time (utilize time-management strategies).

Remember that God is with you in your stressful situation. The following are some key spiritual considerations:

1. It is to our advantage to renew our relationship with God often. In Revelation 2:4, 5 Jesus is talking about how the Church has lost its first love. "Nevertheless I have this against you, that you have left your first love. Remember therefore from where you have fallen; repent and do the first works, or else I will come to you quickly and remove your lampstand from its place—unless you repent."

We may ask ourselves how does this happen? I believe Jesus is saying we let things, other desires and even sinful habits crowd out God: our self-centered pleasure has made our love for God grow cold. For many I have counseled over the years, this has been their spiritual downfall that has created destruction in many areas of their lives and families.

Jesus gives us three key points for restoration. He encourages us to remember what He has done for us in His death and resurrection.

Secondly, we need to repent, to ask God to forgive us for our sins and thirdly to get back to obeying God and serving Him the way we once did.

2. It is imperative that we renew our relationship with ourselves. This is basically finding out who we are in Jesus Christ. The words of Jesus in John 10:27-30 are some of the greatest to show who we are and who we belong to. "My sheep hear My voice, and I know them, and they follow Me. And I give them eternal life, and they shall never perish; neither shall anyone snatch them out of My hand. My Father, who has given them to Me, is greater than all; and no one is able to snatch them out of My Father's hand. I and My Father are one." What beautiful words for the one who struggles with fear, stress and low self esteem. I would recommend you memorize these verses.

3. In the busy world around us and the hectic lives we live, it is easy to neglect our family. We need to renew our relationship with our family. This involves asking forgiveness for being too busy, for being insensitive to your family, and for not putting them first.

4. We need to renew our mind by watching for false guilt. True guilt is from the Holy Spirit who convicts us when we sin. We need to ask God to forgive us and be restored. False guilt comes from three main sources: our own negative thinking; what others say about us; and the accuser of the believer, Satan.

In order to deal with false guilt, strive to keep your mind clear of accusations. Forgive yourself for negative thinking, forgive others for their unjust, unkind statements about you and use the Scriptures. Claim the blood of Christ to defeat the lies of Satan.

Worry, anxiety and fear

Following the death of Elvis Presley, many were shocked to learn of his paranoiac fear. It seems that Elvis was controlled by incapacitating fear from which he could find no release. Those close to him said Elvis had four or five bodyguards with him at all times. He never ate or drank anything unless it was first tasted by someone else; he wouldn't even go to the bathroom alone. In the last months of his life, Elvis was taking eight different kinds of prescription drugs and as many as 25 of them a day. Some medical experts have speculated that the multi-millionaire died from a drug overdose rather than a heart attack.

Presley used drugs to alleviate the all-encompassing fear that captivated his thinking. Millions of people are just like him, suffering from worry, anxiety and fear to a greater or lesser degree.

These three emotions are connected and overlapping concepts. For the sake of clarity, we need to define and explain how worry, anxiety and fear can all lead to one another, and how they can also exist together.

Worry

Worry is that niggling reminder that something is not quite right in our world. Worry often involves future uncertainties. Children worry they won't have friends at school. Adults worry they won't be able to keep their job. We wonder how we'll put away money for our children's education. Will we get that promotion? How will we afford those necessary car repairs? Is my spouse cheating on me? Will we be evicted from our apartment if we can't pay the rent on time?

Worry is experienced emotionally and mentally. It involves thinking...thinking...thinking. Some call this ruminating, a word that comes from the rural example of a cow continually chewing and re-chewing her cud. Thinking like this produces negative emotions that circle back into the worry cycle—all of which can be an exhausting experience that leads to difficulty thinking rationally about the concerns. We can become consumed with the 'what ifs?' Unchecked, worry leads to anxiety and very often, to full-blown fear.

Anxiety

Anxiety involves the same mental ruminating as worry. Instead of sleeping, we may stay awake thinking—well into the morning hours. The unhappy result of this is a lack of adequate rest which only exacerbates the problem by leaving one over-tired and lacking the mental control to manage the worry in a healthy way. Appetite may be affected and the body is deprived of the nutrients it needs for optimum health.

When worry becomes anxiety, the person may experience physical symptoms like a shaky feeling inside, restlessness, tightening of the chest or upper body. Some people feel as if they have butterflies in their stomach.

Anxiety, if not checked, can become chronic. Instead of periodic worrying, the anxiety is there all the time—emotionally, mentally, and sometimes physically. For some people, the anxiety grows until they require medical intervention. Unfortunately, medical intervention alone is not the most effective form of treatment. A more effective way is using the Bible to control the worry that exists in anxiety. The Bible advises us to "have the mind of Christ."

"Let this mind be in you which was also in Christ Jesus" (Philippians 2:5). Jesus gave His concerns to God in prayer, as we see in the account of Jesus in the Garden of Gethsemane where He stated: "Father, if it is Your will, take this cup away from Me; nevertheless not My will, but Yours, be done" (Luke 22:42).

Fear

Sometimes anxiety becomes so great it grows into fear, and fear is another beast altogether. Fear is all-encompassing and all-consuming. The Bible tells us that fear causes torment: "There is no fear in love; but perfect love casts out fear because fear involves torment. But he who fears has not been made perfect in love. We love Him because He first loved us" (1 John 4: 18, 19).

Medical science says there are 287 different fears and phobias that can prevent us from living confident and productive lives. Everyone has some fear. Perhaps it is a fear of doing poorly in school, in sports, or being rejected by a girlfriend or boyfriend. Children at school hear about divorce and ask their mother, "Are you and Daddy getting a divorce?"

After being in a car accident, a person I counseled was afraid to get into a vehicle. Another woman feared riding in a car because her mother was killed in an accident many years before. A woman who grew up in Europe during World War II developed a paralyzing fear of spiders, from having to hide in a narrow dirt tunnel every time the air raid siren sounded. During my years as a foster child, I lived in constant fear of physical abuse and punishment from my foster mother.

Sue, a young Christian, was terrified of death. She obsessed about it and seemed to think about death continuously. When she came to me for counseling, I said, "Sue, do you see that closed door?"

"Yes," she replied.

"Death is like walking through the door and into the arms of our Lord Jesus Christ. As you approach Jesus, He will say, 'Welcome home, Sue,'" I assured her.

In a later session, Sue shared with me how the illustration of Jesus' open arms had completely driven away her fear of death and dying.

Some would like to persuade us that fear, worry, and anxiety are the same thing, but from personal experience, I know that is not true. Anxiety is a negative response to life's agitations. Fear is a total response to the possibility that the worst thing can and will happen.

Fear is universal, and it is crippling. The Bible says that fear is torment created by Satan. Fear is not just a mental quirk, but an evil spirit that emanates from the enemy. Fear can prevent us from reaching out to God. The Bible teaches: "For God has not given us a spirit of fear, but of power and of love and of a sound mind" (2 Timothy 1:7). "For you did not receive the spirit of bondage again to fear, but you received the Spirit of adoption by whom we cry out, 'Abba, Father'" (Romans 8:15).

Believers in Christ have not received a spirit of fear, but the Spirit of adoption by God, and it is with this Biblical principle in hand that I approach every client who has a fear problem.

Fear can be deeply spiritual in nature with an oppressive quality to it. People may experience a fear of the unknown, a dark reality that they cannot name. This is particularly terrorizing, and is often something they won't openly share with family and friends. Nevertheless, it is very real for the individual. Fear of this kind can become so paralyzing that people need support to overcome it. The most effective strategy for overcoming fear of any kind is prayer and God's Word.

Fear causes us to expect the worst

Turn of the century author Ambrose Bierce, wrote a short story that illustrates this perfectly. A man who was afraid of snakes came to visit a friend who had a reptile collection. At the end of the day, the visitor went up to the room he'd been given, and as he was getting ready for bed, he noticed two red eyes shining out from under the bed. He was instantly seized with fear and fell back in a chair behind him.

In the narrative, Bierce goes to great lengths to describe the man's terror and how, too embarrassed to call for help, he remained frozen in the chair, totally incapacitated by what he feared his fate would be. In the middle of the night, his host heard a crash and ran to the man's room to find the chair tipped over and the man lying on the floor, dead of an apparent heart attack. As the host reached down to touch the dead man, he noticed two red eyes under the bed. He reached under and brought out his child's toy snake.

The unfortunate character's fear was real, even though the object of his fear was impotent. But some fears are very valid. Brent, a man I worked with at the Billy Graham Association was a Westerner who used to drive cattle on the range and often slept outdoors under the stars. One night, after climbing into his sleeping bag, he prepared to go to sleep when he felt something slithering into the sleeping bag with him. It was a rattlesnake. My friend knew that any attempt on his part to exit the sleeping bag could alarm the rattler and invite a fatal bite. His only option was to lie perfectly still all night long, until the warmth of the morning sun lured the snake out of the bag. Although Brent's fear was real, he was able to overcome by resisting the compulsion to move. For many individuals, fear has become debilitating in their lives because they refuse to face it and allow Christ to free them.

My own fear in boyhood was the fear of a negative outcome. I was afraid of the physical punishment my foster mother would deal out totally unexpectedly and often for no apparent reason. My brother and I lived in a constant state of fear, but because of our different personalities, we reacted differently. My brother withdrew while I attacked. Of course, my attacks were not on the person I wanted to attack (the foster mother); they were displaced upon whomever I felt had wronged me at the moment.

What We Focus On Controls Us

If we focus on a fear, that fear will soon control our emotions, our thoughts, and our actions, and keep us from living in trust and peace.

A perfect example of this happened one night when a strange noise outside roused me from sleep. The sound seemed to be coming from the backyard. Was it an intruder, I wondered, a thief about to break into our house?

Rather than put my head under the covers, I decided to face my fears. After all, I had a family to protect. I got out of bed and tiptoed quietly to the backdoor where the noise seemed to be. As I cautiously peeked out, I noticed that the screen door was swinging back and forth. Deeply relieved, I pulled it shut.

However, as I closed the inside door and was about to go back to bed, I noticed a faint light in the basement. It was a light I'd never seen before. It seemed rather like the beam of a flashlight. Had someone broken into the house after all? My knees were shaky, but I knew I had to investigate. There was no use going back to bed.

I eased down the stairs, trying to make as little noise as possible. By the time I reached the bottom, my heart pounded like a jackhammer. I peeked around the corner, fully expecting to see an intruder, yet knowing I had no idea what I would do when I confronted him.

There was no intruder. The light came from Fern's sewing machine, which she had forgotten to turn off.

As I climbed the stairs and headed for bed (relieved beyond description), I couldn't help but reflect on how easily our fears can control us. Even after I got into bed, the thought kept coming, "Oh yeah? You think you've explained the light, but what if you're wrong? Maybe there really is someone down there. You'd better go down and check again."

I could have spent all night thinking about it, unable to sleep. Instead, I prayed against the spirit of fear. I said, "In the name of the Lord Jesus Christ, Son of God, I rebuke the evil spirit of fear that is plaguing my mind." In a very short time I had fallen asleep.

I have counseled clients who were afraid to leave their house. They would stand at the window and peak through a crack in the drapes, afraid to go out for fear something might happen to them. Their fear was crippling them both mentally and socially.

I once counseled a woman who was so afraid of the dark she dreaded going to sleep, in case someone might enter her house and harm her. She didn't allow herself sleep until it began to get light, and then she would only sleep for a few hours. In winter, when the nights are long, she hardly slept at all.

In our sessions, we began to talk about where this fear originates. Often the person is unsure. For others it will be the memory of a father, a grandfather, a brother coming into the room in the dark and sexually abusing them. In one case, it was an older brother who locked a little sister in the basement as a practical joke. The brother would torment her with stories of snakes and other frightening creatures. Throughout her lifetime Brigette was afraid of dark places and was concerned that she would be restrained or locked up in a tight dark space. This was one of the presenting problems at the first counseling session.

Men and women who have been sexually abused have a deep-seated fear of men (and sometimes women). It can get to the point where, whenever they encounter an adult, they immediately withdraw. Their fear makes them feel physically sick inside. They may become nauseated and unable to eat. Or they may overeat, and not exercise. Often they deliberately neglect themselves. One woman told me, "I stay fat and stinky so my dad and brothers won't sexually abuse me."

Fear affects us spiritually. It can lead to questioning God and demanding, "Where are You? Why won't you take away my fear?"

Uncontrolled fear becomes a stronghold in a person's life, resulting in sleeplessness, depression, and nervous breakdowns. There is a direct correlation between ongoing fear and depression.

Fearful People in the Bible

There are numerous examples of fearful people in the Bible. Jacob, who cheated his twin Esau of his birthright and his rightful blessing, was understandably fearful of Esau when Jacob returned to his home after many years of self-imposed exile in a distant country.

How could teen-aged Joseph not have been filled with fear after his brothers stripped him and threw him in a well? He had to be even more fearful when he was sold as a slave and taken by strangers into a foreign land.

In the Psalms, David often expressed his fear and his sense of help-lessness during his years on the run from King Saul who made no secret of the fact he meant to kill David.

Even Jesus admitted His dread of the cup of suffering in the Garden of Gethsemane when He begged God, His Father, to take that cup from Him. However, Jesus submitted to His Father's wishes by saying, "… nevertheless, not My will, but Yours, be done."

There was a point when the famous American merchant, J. C. Penny, was consumed with fear. The stock market had crashed and everything around him was collapsing. His business was in ruins; his health was gone, and Penny was convinced he was going to die. But as he lay in his hospital bed one Sunday morning waiting for the end to come, from the chapel down the hall came the sound of a choir singing, "God will take care of you…" God spoke to J. C. Penny in that moment and removed his fear. From that day on, the words of the hymn became Penny's motto, and he went on to establish the department store empire that still bears his name.

Going Back To Go Ahead

When dealing with people who are in captivity because of a particular fear, I encourage them to go back to go ahead. I ask them to go back in their memory to see where their particular fear began. People are often told to forget their fear—to "just get over it" and move on. I say, no. Go back. Identify the specific fear. Identify where it started. Identify what created that fear. Isolate the fear. Say what it is. Name it.

In some cases, the person won't know where the fear began, so we begin working back together. Janet, a woman in her early fifties, came to me for help because she was consumed by fear. Many of her fears were unfounded, yet she was incapable of gaining victory over them. Her greatest fear was of water. Even having a bath, a shower, or drinking a glass of cold water could make her panic. Janet related one incident where she was to have a shower and wash her hair at her daughter's place, but because of this deep-seated fear of water, Janet insisted her daughter stay right outside the shower door until she was finished.

It was quite obvious that an incident earlier in her life had pre-cipitated the unnatural fear, so I asked Janet to think back. Could she think of any one incident that might have made her afraid of water? She remembered an event that took place in Europe more than forty years prior. Janet related how, as a young child unable to swim, she was pushed into a swimming pool. She could not recall how she was rescued or who rescued her.

I prayed for emotional or inner healing for Janet. I asked Jesus Christ to go back and remove the emotional hurts, scars or fears that Janet was unable to overcome. I asked Jesus to return to that particular town in Europe where Janet was pushed into the pool and set her free from the bondage that had rendered her helpless for so many years.

Often I ask clients to concentrate on the Lord Jesus Christ and His love while I'm praying. I had asked Janet to do this, and afterward she related how, while I was praying, she saw herself drowning in a pool. She sensed a tremendous wave of panic engulfing her, but as the prayer continued, she felt the presence of Christ and His strong arms lifting her to safety. Janet was freed from her fear of water.

When dealing with clients like Janet with very crippling fear issues, I first discover where they are in their relationship with Jesus Christ. Then we develop a spiritual program to deal with that. A spiritual program for Janet and others would consist of scriptural passages to read each day, and specific verses to memorize that speak of overcoming fear. I give them an assignment to write down other situations that provoked fear in their lives from the past or present and then bring the list to the next counseling session, so we can pray through it.

Many times I will encourage clients to read through the four Gospels and take special note of the words Jesus used for comfort, peace and security. I recently asked a businessman I was counseling—who had struggled with fear most of his life—to read Psalm 139 and the first chapter of Ephesians. We took the time to work through the passages. Jackson realized that his worth came from God. I have some clients do a critique on a book that I believe would be helpful.

We talk about fear extinction and examine verses in the Bible that speak to fear. Although psychologists have used that term in the Behaviour Modification literature, I have found it helpful for clients to change their fearful, angry, resentful behaviour with the use of scripture and practical exercises.

Jason, for example, had a great fear of elevators and would walk up long sets of stairs to avoid the trauma of being confined to an elevator. The fear extinction program would consist of scriptural passages and verses to be read every day and, in particular, just prior to facing the giant called fear. I have used this spiritual exercise for clients in a city center mall that has many floors and an active elevator. With the scriptures in mind, they are told to start and stop at the entrance the first day. The following day they move inside. The next, they sit on the bench in front of the elevator. The fear extinction process continues until they are able to consistently ride the elevator whenever they wish.

Verses to Conquer Fear

The power of reading and quoting God's Word gives one the courage and freedom to defeat the fear. "He gives power to the weak, and to those who have no might He increases strength. Even the youths shall faint and be weary, and the young men shall utterly fall: But those who wait on the Lord shall renew their strength; they shall mount up with wings like eagles, they shall run, and not be weary; they shall walk and not faint" (Isaiah 40:29-31).

"Fear not, for I am with you; Be not dismayed, for I am your God. I will strengthen you, Yes, I will help you, I will uphold you with My righteous right hand.' "Behold, all those who were incensed against you shall be ashamed and disgraced; They shall be as nothing, And those who strive with you shall perish. You shall seek them and not find them—Those who contended with you. Those who war against you shall be as nothing, As a nonexistent thing. For I, the LORD your God, will hold your right hand, saying to you, 'Fear not, I will help you. "Fear not, you worm Jacob, You men of Israel! I will help you," says the LORD And your Redeemer, the Holy One of Israel. (Isaiah 41: 10-14).

"Rejoice in the Lord always: and again I say, rejoice. Let your moderation be known unto all men. The Lord is at hand. Be careful for nothing; but in everything by prayer and supplication with thanksgiving let your requests be made known unto God. And the peace of God, which passeth all understanding, shall keep your hearts and minds through Christ Jesus" (Philippians 4:4-7, KJV).

"You will keep him in perfect peace whose mind is stayed on You, Because he trusts in You" (Isaiah 26:3).

Jennifer, who had been in and out of psychiatric care, came to me for help. She and her husband were at Bible college, preparing for the ministry, but she felt overwhelmed with fear. The fear went back to a night when her husband was away working at a job to put himself through school. A man broke into their apartment and, with a knife to her throat, Jennifer was raped. Because of the traumatic experience, Jennifer was filled with fear and guilt that she was not fit to work with her husband in ministry. We prayed for emotional healing, and God took away her fear and guilt. "Fear not, for I am with you; Be not dismayed, for I am your God. I will strengthen you, Yes, I will help you. I will uphold you with My righteous right hand" (Isaiah 41:10).

I met Gerald, a businessman, at a men's retreat. When he learned I was a professional counselor, he was eager to talk. I suggested we go for a walk together. The man was very wealthy and appeared to have every success, yet he struggled with the fear of failure. I encouraged him to go back to go forward. He had no trouble recognizing that his fear began when he was young and his father told him, "You'll never amount to anything, and nobody will ever marry you." Even though he had proven his father wrong, this man was still consumed with the fear that he would ultimately fail. We prayed for his emotional healing, and some time later, he sent me a card with a note saying, "Thank you....What a wonderful thing to be out of prison."

"For God has not given us a spirit of fear, but of power and of love and of a sound mind" (2 Timothy 1:7).

When the Physical is Involved

Richard was married, had several children, and was involved in youth work, but he was so consumed by fear that he couldn't even drive the car by himself. Whenever he drove, his breath grew laboured, and he had heart palpitations, trembling, and fear of passing out behind the wheel. Whether Richard needed to go to a youth rally out of town or to a meeting just across the city, he always insisted his wife come along. Though he'd felt afraid, insecure and inferior all his life, this fear of driving had not become a problem until recently—just about the time he committed himself to serving the Lord.

When he arrived at my office, Richard looked the epitome of defeat, an individual who had given up all hope of finding freedom from his fear. He felt tremendous guilt because his wife had to take care of him, be with him, and pamper him. Richard was resentful because he wanted to serve God, but had been reduced to impotence in every area of his life.

I helped Richard understand that the fear plaguing him was not from God, but from Satan, as Romans 8:15 and 1 Timothy 1:7 teach. I assigned verses to overcome fear for Richard to review and memorize to help him in this battle. I also advised him to be aware of Satan's attacks and to refer to Ephesians 6, where Paul reminds believers to recognize the enemy's strategies and go to God for the strength to resist.

"Finally, my brethren, be strong in the Lord, and in the power of His might. Put on the whole armor of God that you may be able to stand against the wiles of the devil. For we wrestle not against flesh and blood, but against principalities, against powers, against the rulers of the darkness of this world, against spiritual hosts of wickedness in heavenly places" (Ephesians 6: 10–12).

Richard needed to realize that the battle was already won if he would let Christ help him in his fight.

When I learned that depression, frequent mood swings, and violent reactions to overindulgence in sweets were also a major part of Richard's dilemma, I suspected he might be suffering from hypoglycemia, which is a condition of low blood sugar.

Psychological by-products of hypoglycemia can include inability to concentrate, depression, irritability, anxiety, excessive fears that have no real basis, disorientation, fatigue, insomnia, perceptual and thought disturbances, and hostility. A medical doctor confirmed Richard's hypoglycemia and put him on a high protein/low carbohydrate diet supplemented with Vitamin B and C therapy.

As Richard was faithful to the hypoglycemic diet and to prayer and Bible study, and to binding Satan's power over his life and the renunciation of his fear, guilt, and depression, he experienced freedom within three months. To overcome his fear of driving alone and being with people in groups, I encouraged Richard to force himself to be involved in those activities to demonstrate God's power over his fears. I let Richard know that he would have to work hard on those things all his life. If he is not consistent, he could get right back to where he began.

It is sad, but true that some people start well, but quit too soon.

What We Believe About Jesus Christ Will Dictate How We Live Our Life

If I focused only on the mistreatment I received as a child in the foster home, I would never have moved on. If I focused on my dad's alcoholism and his immorality, I would never have moved on. Only when I focused on Jesus Christ and His healing power was I able to move forward in my life.

Moving forward is crucial, because we will stay stuck in the past with thoughts that are destructive. Let me explain by this story:

A Christian medical doctor asked me to visit a pastor who was in the hospital, near death. He was afraid to die. During my conversation with the pastor, I tried to get to the root of his fear. He wouldn't tell me specifically, but he did admit that something had happened when he was seventeen for which he did not believe God would ever forgive him. Sadly, this man had carried on a ministry for many, many years without feeling that he himself would ever be accepted into Heaven. "Did you ask God to forgive you for what happened back there?" I asked.

"Hundreds of times," he said.

I told him, "You only had to ask once." I read him 1 John 1:9. "If we confess our sins, He is faithful and just to forgive us our sins and to cleanse us from all unrighteousness." I said, "You asked God to forgive you and He has. Now you have to forgive yourself for whatever happened."

We prayed through that time in his life; the man accepted God's forgiveness, chose to forgive himself and was set free.

Carrie experienced fear all her life. She was so fearful she was powerless to do virtually anything. Fear gripped her over the smallest things, and had a tyrannical hold on her even though Carrie had been a believer in Christ for many years.

Carrie's father was a Christian, but was also a perfectionist who had a violent temper that often exploded out of control. Carrie's fear probably began in early childhood when her father, in a fit of anger, dealt harshly with her.

I became involved with Carrie's case about the time she needed a gallbladder operation. Given the situation and her propensity for fear, Carrie naturally expected the worst. She feared it was not a gallbladder problem, but cancer. She rejected the opinion of her doctor (a Christian) that this was not cancer, and continued to be convinced that she would either die from her cancer or have a nervous breakdown. (The latter seemed possible since Carrie had a relative who had experienced mental problems.)

Carrie phoned me many times from her hospital room for counsel. Physically, she had recovered very well after the gallbladder operation, but mentally and emotionally she was a wreck. After not sleeping for six nights despite an abundance of sleeping pills and tranquilizers, Carrie figured she had three options: keep struggling over a mental breakdown; commit suicide; or drive to my office for emergency counseling. Fortunately, she chose the latter.

My first strategy with Carrie was to present scripture that had to do with victory over fear, the abundant life, and the power of Jesus Christ, the Holy Spirit and the Word of God. Carrie said she couldn't believe it: she had too many fears, doubts and worries. God brought to my mind the verse from 2 Timothy 2:13: "If we are faithless, He remains faithful; He cannot deny Himself." I told Carrie that no matter what she believed, God promised He would not go back on His Word, and if He said so, we must believe it and act on it.

Since Carrie's problem was so severe, I called in some other Christians to pray with us, but still Carrie remained in bondage. After more prayer, the Lord impressed some teaching from James 5 on my mind: "Is any sick among you? Let him call for the elders of the church; and let them pray over him, anointing him with oil in the name of the Lord. And the prayer of faith shall save the sick, and the Lord shall raise him up..." (James 5:14, 15 KJV).

After reading that passage and others that spoke of Jesus' healing ministry, we prayed and anointed Carrie with oil. Carrie describes what happened next: "I was sitting on the chesterfield, and he anointed me with oil. While he was still praying, Jesus took my body and laid me down and all other things just left me. All I could think of doing was looking into His eyes and praising Him. I had never had a power like that come over me, from that day to this day. Jesus is so real in my life. He assures me every minute that He is with me."

Over the next weeks, Carrie faithfully pursued the spiritual program I gave her of Bible study, praising God, and memorizing scripture passages. She began to share her story and minister to others.

Today, Carrie is a vibrant, confident believer who has helped many other people to experience the same love, joy, and peace that Jesus Christ gave her. She has also been able to counsel members of her family who experienced traumatic difficulties.

Changing Our Focus From Fear To The Spiritual

The most effective step in achieving lasting freedom from stress, worry, anxiety and fear is to change our focus from our fear to a personal relationship with Jesus Christ. Fear can easily become a stronghold; Christ is the only One who can pull down the stronghold, but we must let Him. The Bible says, "For though we walk in the flesh, we do not war according to the flesh. For the weapons of our warfare are not carnal, but mighty in God for pulling down strongholds, casting down arguments and every high thing that exalts itself against the knowledge of God, bringing every thought into captivity to the obedience of Christ (2 Corinthians 10:3-5).

This means that in ourselves, we have no weapons that can pull down the emotional strongholds. We need God's almighty power to destroy our bad thinking and, in this case, our fears. We need God to have control of our minds and emotions. We need to change our thinking from a focus on our hurt and pain, and fill our minds with scripture instead. We need to focus on what God says, instead of what we have been thinking. "You will keep him in perfect peace whose mind is stayed on You, Because he trusts in You" (Isaiah 26:3). Focusing on the spiritual dimension means focusing on prayer and on the words of God in scripture. "Call upon me in the day of trouble; I will deliver you and you shall glorify Me" (Psalm 50: 15).

We must call upon Him. Sometimes a client will say to me, "Yes, I know all that. I've done it, but nothing has changed." Nothing will change until that person becomes actively involved in his own healing. Involvement means telling God what your problem is. That's what it means to call upon God. It means praying specifically and saying: "God,

I'm in trouble." "I've been hurt." "My marriage is in trouble." "My parents are getting a divorce." "I've lost my job."

Involvement also means doing the homework, praying and forgiving others and doing it willingly and wholeheartedly. Without that, no healing will take place. As a counselor, I can't change anyone's life; I'm just a facilitator. God gives the healing, but the client has to be involved.

Occasionally when I'm speaking to a client, encouraging him to participate actively in his healing, he will say, "I can't." To me, that means that either he does not know how to, or will not. If clients don't know how, I can teach them and lead them to victory. Very rarely have individuals refused to try. Once that is established, it is easy to have them agree to homework that will help them to overcome their fears. This passage in Philippians is one that I encourage people to memorize and put into practise every day: "Be anxious for nothing, but in everything by prayer and supplication, with thanksgiving, let your requests be made known to God, and the peace of God, which surpasses all understanding, will guard your hearts and minds through Christ Jesus. Finally, brethren, whatever things are true, whatever things are noble, whatever things are just, whatever things are pure, whatever things are lovely, whatever things are of good report, if there is any virtue and if there is anything praiseworthy—meditate on these things" (Philippians 4:6-8).

We are blessed as followers of Christ to have at least five reasons not to fear, that He Himself offered to us. Let us examine Christ's beautiful words of comfort which gives us peace.

Five Reasons Not To Fear
In Revelation 1: 17 and 18, Jesus gives us five reasons not to fear: "And when I saw Him, I fell at His feet as dead. But He laid His right hand on me, saying to me, 'Do not be afraid; I am the First and the Last. I am He who lives, and was dead, and behold, I am alive forever more. Amen. And I have the keys of Hades and Death.'"

Reason #1:
Jesus said, "I am the First and the Last." He had the first word and will have the last word. Everything is controlled by Him. We need to accept Jesus Christ as Lord. If you haven't yet done that, call up a friend who

has, or a pastor of a local church, and explain your need and desire. They can help you. You can pray this prayer on your own. Say, "Lord Jesus I need you. I ask you to come into my life and save me. Please forgive all of my sin and help me to live for you. I thank you Jesus for hearing me."

Reason #2:

Jesus said, "I am He who lives." He chose to be an authentic living being for a space of thirty-three years. He was conceived by the Holy Spirit within Mary, and we are not to fear because Jesus lived a human life. Jesus was confronted with many of the same issues we are today. He won the victory by having constant communion with His heavenly Father. He gave us this example that we are to follow. God the Father's perfect love drives away our fear as we recognize nothing happens in our life as His children, without His knowledge and His permission. The passage in Philippians emphasised this very thing: "Let this mind be in you which was also in Christ Jesus, who, being in the form of God, did not consider it robbery to be equal with God, but made Himself of no reputation, taking the form of a bondservant, and coming in the likeness of men, and being found in appearance as a man, He humbled Himself and became obedient to the point of death, even the death of the cross. Therefore God also has highly exalted Him and given Him the name which is above every name, that at the name of Jesus every knee would bow, of those in heaven and of those on earth and of those under the earth, and that every tongue should confess that Jesus Christ is Lord, to the glory of God the Father" (Philippians 2:5-11).

We should not fear, because Jesus lived a human life of victory by doing everything His Heavenly Father asked Him to do and never sinned.

Reason #3:

We should not fear because Jesus' sole purpose was to come to die as our sacrifice unto salvation. So Christ hung on the cross for us and paid the penalty for our sin. We who have accepted Christ's payment for us will never have to face eternal separation from God, because Jesus' death was the bridge to the Father. We are to rejoice because the fear of death is removed. (1 Cor. 15:56, 57)

Reason #4:
Jesus said, "I am alive forevermore. Amen." After three days and three nights in the tomb, He arose, never to die again. Today He ever lives to make intercession for us and asks us to come to Him. "Come unto Me, all you who labor and are heavy laden, and I will give you rest" (Matthew 11:28). "Therefore He is also able to save to the uttermost those who come to God through Him, since He always lives to make intercession for them" (Hebrews 7:25).

Reason #5:
Jesus has the keys of Hell and death. This means that all who have accepted Christ as their Saviour will not be rejected, but will go to live with Him in Heaven forever. Therefore, there is no reason to fear anything that may assail us in our life. "Yet in all these things we are more than conquerors through Him who loved us. For I am persuaded that neither death nor life, nor angels nor principalities nor powers, nor things present nor things to come, nor height nor depth, nor any other created thing, shall be able to separate us from the love of God which is in Christ Jesus our Lord" (Romans 8:37-39).

Prayer
"I know Your Word says, "The Lord is my light and my salvation—whom shall I fear? The Lord is the stronghold of my life—of whom shall I be afraid?" (Psalm 27:1) But Lord, I have existed with fears and the emotional torture of anxiety and worry for days, months and even years. Forgive me for believing the worries of my life are stronger and more potent than the Almighty, All-powerful, All-knowing God who is the Captain of heaven's armies. I look to You, Lord, as the source for my emotional deliverance. In Your Word and on Your character I will trust, for 'the Lord gives strength to His people; the Lord blesses His people with peace' (Psalm 29:11)."

Chapter 5: I Love to Hate: Unforgiveness, Bitterness and Hatred

Years ago, I was flying out of Yellowknife in the Northwest Territories of Canada, where I had conducted a weekend of seminars. Our flight path took us over the Giant Mine, where just days before an explosion had killed nine workers.

Just seeing the site gave me an eerie feeling, perhaps because I knew the explosion was deliberately set. Roger Warren was the man responsible. He was motivated by bitterness over an ongoing work dispute that resulted in the regular workers being shut out and replacement workers being brought in. Roger had become so resentful and bitter that he decided to take matters into his own hands. Carrying concealed explosives, he slipped past the guards and planted the explosives in the mine. He wanted the attention of the mine administration. He didn't realize a shift of replacement workers had just begun.

Roger Warren ultimately went to trial and was convicted in the deaths of the nine replacement workers and given a life sentence—all because of unrestrained bitterness.

What is bitterness?
Bitterness is anger that has been nurtured and prolonged. I would add, nurtured by unforgiveness. Bitterness will ultimately result in hatred. Dr.

S. I. MacMillan, in his book *None of These Diseases*, provides an excellent commentary on the power of hatred.

MacMillan writes, "The moment I start hating a man, I become his slave. I can't enjoy my work anymore; he even controls my thoughts. My resentments produce too many stress hormones in my body and I'm fatigued after only a few hours of work. The work I formerly enjoyed is now drudgery. Even vacations cease to give me pleasure. It may be a luxurious car that I drive along a lake fringed by the autumnal beauty of maple, oak and birch. As far as my experience of pleasure is concerned, I might as well be driving a wagon in mud and rain. The man I hate hounds me wherever I go. I can't escape his tyrannical grasp on my mind. When the waiter serves me a porterhouse steak with French fries, asparagus, salad and strawberry shortcake smothered with ice cream, it might as well be stale bread and water. My teeth chew it and I swallow it, but the man I hate will not permit me to enjoy it" (Page 72).

MacMillan could just as easily have written "the man I'm bitter toward" instead of "the man I hate." The two are interchangeable.

The writer goes on to say that prolonged bitterness can generate a whole range of diseases and conditions. Science has proven that bitterness thins out the bones and breaks down the immune system, leaving the body susceptible to at least forty different diseases.

There is also a correlation between the negative emotions of jealousy, bitterness, and hatred. Jealousy, if not dealt with, can lead to bitterness which is an inward emotion. Hatred is its outward expression.

In my professional experience I have seen unrestrained bitterness manifest itself in a variety of destructive behaviours like eating disorders, alcoholism, drugs, sexual promiscuity, and other obsessive-compulsive behaviour.

What causes bitterness?

Many things can bring on bitterness. Shame, abuse, put-downs and ridicule at home or on the playground in childhood—all have an impact. Unfair treatment and blocked goals can also be a cause. Some people in business are jealous of their employers because they haven't reached the same high position of power or influence. When they are unable to advance as they would like to, they become bitter.

I experienced very deep bitterness as a child. I was particularly bitter because my brother and I had been wrenched away from our mother and dumped in the abusive foster home. Not only could we not be with our parents, we couldn't even see them. As the years went on, there was bitterness and resentment at the constant reminder we were unwanted foster kids. I was bitter about not being able to do what I wanted to do—the things all my friends were doing. And I was bitter against God because, as I saw it, He killed my foster dad when the one I wanted God to kill was my foster mother.

My bitterness was so overwhelming and so controlling it was like being enclosed in a dense fog. It made me want to lash out constantly against the unfairness of it all and the people I viewed as being responsible—mostly my foster mother.

Failure can also result in being bitter toward one's self. While teaching at the University, I had the opportunity to speak with Patricia, a young woman who was failing her classes and was angry and bitter at herself because of her lifestyle. She spent too much time partying and not enough time studying. Her hardworking parents had spent a lot of money to enable her to go to university to study for what they hoped would be a teaching career. Patricia was bitter at herself because of her own failure. Her marks were suffering. She told me that she hated herself so much there were many times she thought of jumping off a bridge and ending her life.

Thankfully, Patricia was able to get on track spiritually by embracing a relationship with Jesus Christ and asking God's forgiveness. She also forgave herself and began applying herself to her studies. Her marks improved. Within a few years Patricia had that teaching certificate. Patricia could easily have been destroyed by her bitterness at her own failure to perform. Instead she was able to find freedom in the love of God.

In many cases, individuals are bitter because there is conditional love in a marriage, the home, or the church. Conditional love says, "I love you ...if you perform. I love you...if you do a good job. I love you...if you meet my needs."

Conditional love is based on performance and one's own feelings, rather than the unconditional love that truly ministers to those we're supposed to care about. At some time or another, we have all been guilty of practicing conditional love.

I have worked with many clients who are bitter toward their parents. Perhaps they were never quite good enough to suit the mother or father; they didn't achieve high enough marks, or were lacking in some way. These people had all experienced love that was conditional. They had to earn it.

Remember Charlotte from an earlier chapter who felt rejected and abandoned because she was never accepted by her father in the same way as her sister? When the sister died, the father said, "I wish it was you who died. Your sister was pretty and you're ugly." Charlotte's bitterness was patently evident and, frankly, quite understandable. She had suffered ridicule, put-downs, and abuse from a person who should have been her protector and her best encourager.

I think of Gloria who struggled in school because of her whole home environment. She buried her hatred of her mother and dad in anger and bitterness. Now her marriage was beginning to deteriorate as she struggled in the area of love and intimacy. She was like a volcano about to erupt.

During one session, I suggested we do some role-playing. She would be herself. I would play the role of her mother. I began to make some of the deeply hurtful statements her mother had made to her. As we dialogued back and forth, Gloria actually got out of her chair and came toward me with her hands outstretched, ready to wrap them around my throat. Of course, I halted the dialogue immediately and brought Gloria's response to her attention. Her feelings of hurt, pain, and bitterness—results of all the shame she had experienced—were bursting out of the deep place where she had tried to bury that shame.

Gloria learned to bring to Christ the bitterness she felt over her home environment, and the verbal and emotional abuse she had suffered. She came to the place where she was able to forgive family members and move forward. By coming to a relationship with God and Jesus Christ, and recognizing that God had forgiven her, Gloria could forgive her family. If she had not dealt with the shame that created so much bitterness in her life, I believe she would have committed suicide or become involved in destructive behaviours. Instead, Gloria was able to find freedom in the love of God.

Angie was married and the mother of several children. She came to the office in a state of anxiety, fear, and depression. Angie had just lost a baby through miscarriage and was painfully bitter. I began talking to her about how God the Father would help her through this.

She reared back her head and exclaimed, "Father! Don't talk to me about 'father'! Let me tell you how my father treated me." And she went on to relate how, as a child, when Angie wanted something from her dad, he would reply, "Say please." When she said, "Please," then he would tell her, "Say pretty please." Then he would make her say, "Pretty please, with sugar on it." This verbal game would go on for some time, and at the end, the father would deny her request anyway—with no explanation given. Angie would be frustrated to the point of tears. Although Angie knew she should love her father, she had deep resentment toward him. As she grew older, she transferred this resentment and bitterness onto God.

The loss of her baby was devastating, but I also realized that a good deal of Angie's depression had to do with her past. We began to work from there to uncover the tremendous hurts she had experienced.

Although Angie had committed her life to Jesus Christ and attended church, she did not have a personal relationship with Christ—the kind of relationship that was a living, growing priority in her life—where she felt loved and transformed by her Saviour.

She was very reluctant to make any further commitment to God because she feared and resented Him. She mentally connected God with her human father. During our sessions, Angie was able to work through her lifetime of hurts and gradually to trust her heavenly Father.

Reading a book about emotional healing was part of Angie's homework. She read parts of it, but said the book brought back too many painful memories. I told Angie the purpose of reading the book was to help her overcome the emotional scars of her past. I also encouraged her, as an act of will rather than feelings, to forgive her father for the way he mistreated her. I assured Angie if she could overcome that hurdle, she would have freedom.

Angie was very reluctant to release her bitterness toward God and her father, but as the sessions continued, and she began to recognize and experience God's love for her, she was able grow in self-acceptance. Her self-image improved, and Angie began to develop a quiet, gentle spirit.

Some people just have a propensity for becoming bitter over insignificant things. That's probably because there are unmet needs somewhere in their life, and the little thing ends up being just the thing that they focus on and grow increasingly bitter. Bitterness also flourishes when other people don't or won't stand with us for a cause. When that happens, we tend to shift blame. At the end of Roger Warren's trial for the gold mine explosion that killed nine people, he blamed everyone else. He blamed the company. He blamed the replacement workers. He said the union was at fault because it didn't protect him and stand with him. Blaming someone else for our bitterness is a common and harmful practice.

Lack of acceptance also causes bitterness. Even in Christian work, people can become bitter when others are chosen instead of them. I have worked with pastors who are deeply bitter because they were replaced. They are bitter against the church because they believe they were just as good as the chosen candidate, and there was no reason for the replacement. Some have been so bitter they have had to look for a job other than pastoring. In cases where the pastor has moved on to shepherd another church, the new congregation has had to deal with his bitterness.

Sometimes the members of the congregation are bitter against the pastor or the church board because of something that has taken place, or some decision that has been made. There are bitter people who go from one church to another, and another, with a chip on their shoulder. They refuse to fit in because of underlying bitterness that may go back a very long time—sometimes even to a negative encounter with a long-ago Sunday school teacher.

Symptoms of bitterness
The symptoms of bitterness are very important to recognize and consider. One overt symptom is complaining about circumstances.

I can't count the number of wives who come for counseling complaining about a lack of love from their husbands. This is always a sure indicator that bitterness resides inside one of the spouses, and sometimes both spouses. As a marriage and family counselor, I try to work with the husband as well. In most cases, the wife is not being loved and appreciated, built up or ministered to as she should be. The husband is too involved with his own needs and pleasures.

Complaining about circumstances often comes to the forefront in group settings. We hear people griping and complaining about others, generally about something that was done to or against them.

Aaron, a young farmer who came to the counseling office for help, griped and complained about everything. It was very obvious Aaron was filled with resentment toward his dad.

"According to my dad," he said bitterly, "I can't, and never could, do anything right."

His father would say, "You can't do that. You're too stupid," or "You're useless. Let me do it," or "Can't you do anything right?"

Understandably, the remarks pierced Aaron's heart like a knife and continued to haunt him into adulthood, even though he had proven himself a very capable and competent farmer.

Another symptom of bitterness is the inability to get along with other people. We see this frequently in churches where individuals drift from church to church and are critical—even abusive—toward the leadership. None of the churches measure up to what they're looking for, even though others in the church find the ministry powerful and refreshing.

Unrealistic expectations are another indicator of bitterness. Bitter people become too hard on themselves, expecting that everything should go well because of the careful way they manage their life. I know of many Christians who expect to be protected from losses in finances, health, job layoff, car breakdowns, or issues around the house or in the family. Unrealistic expectations give rise to bitterness in an individual.

An inability to trust is another symptom of underlying bitterness.

It is easy to understand why individuals who have been abused will not trust anyone. I vividly recall counseling Mary, a woman who had been abused by many men including her grandfather, father, and brothers. "You're a man," Mary challenged me. "Why should I trust you?"

"If I were in your position, I wouldn't trust a man, either," I said.

That honest statement helped her open up. Mary was able to share the horrible physical and sexual abuse she had endured. We were able to proceed with helping her find healing.

A classic symptom of bitterness is denial. Many times in counseling I have stated to a client that he seems angry and bitter. For me it has been hard to miss; bitterness exudes from everything they say. It may be difficult at first for the person to accept that truth, but as we begin going through some of the things they have shared, they are able to acknowledge that, yes, they are bitter and angry.

Bitterness is often characterized by a lack of gratitude. Bitter people are ungrateful people. They have an angry approach to life and behave in a condescending way toward the people around them. The reason why they are so ungrateful is because bitterness makes them so consumed with self-centeredness that others have to bear the wrath of their hostility. A good counseling assignment is to have them practise gratitude to overcome that bitter spirit that controls them.

Bitterness and Unforgiveness

Bitterness often stems from unforgiveness. I have worked with many people who are still bitter toward their spouse even though the husband or wife passed away years before.

A television program some years ago on the topic of divorce caught my attention. Bitterness was a recurring theme in the statements of those interviewed. One woman said, "I'm divorced and my ex-husband is dead, but I'm still angry at him." Another said, "I hate my ex. He was the worst man in town. Do I want to forgive him? Never! Do I really want to harm another person? Yes! I'd like to kill him." Yet another declared, "He broke a sacred promise to me and to God. I'd have to be out of my mind to forgive him!"

How often do we hear the phrase, "I don't get mad; I get even." I've even heard: "To err is human; to forgive is out of the question."

It is imperative to understand that unforgiveness is not a harmless choice, feeling or passion. Unforgiveness can erode a person's mind, heart and soul and cause untold damage. What's worse, a refusal to forgive seems to deepen with time, rather than fade.

Unforgiveness chains us to our past; its destructive effects can pass from generation to generation, and the best and only effective way to stop it is to forgive. But forgiveness is difficult because it goes against our very nature.

A man called to a phone-in program to talk about his 85-year-old neighbour who had been bitter toward him for forty-two years—ever since the man was bitten by the lady's dog and had the dog impounded. She got the dog back, he said, but she is still bitter and calls him up every day to harass him and will continue to do so until the day she dies. She's been taken to court about this and says she is willing to go to jail, if necessary, but she refuses to forgive.

Fred came to my office with chronic depression. After talking with him at length, I said, "The reason you're depressed is because you're a bitter man." He was shocked. He had been in treatment regarding his depression for thirty years and had even seen numerous doctors and psychiatrists, but not one had ever told him that.

I advised Fred he needed to forgive all the people who had caused him pain. Fred did have some genuine hurts from his past, from business, and from the church.

When I told him that, Fred looked doubtful. "Some of them are already dead," he said.

"Doesn't matter," I replied. "I forgave my mom and dad after they passed away."

Fred began to pray. After two weeks, he said he'd never felt so free in all his life. That is what forgiveness does. I still bump into Fred from time to time, even though this is now decades later. He is still happy and content and I can still see the fruit of the work God and Fred did years ago.

Bitterness in the Bible

There are many characters in the Bible who exhibited the deeply destructive emotion of bitterness and its consequences.

We encounter bitterness in two characters in the book of Esther. The first is King Ahasuerus (King Xerxes I) of Persia who threw a massive party for all his officials, servants, nobles and the princes of his kingdom which stretched from India to Ethiopia. After many days of unrestrained drinking, Ahasuerus summoned his Queen to appear before the gathering wearing her royal crown. He wanted to show off her beauty to the people and the officials. She refused.

In his fury and bitterness, Ahasuerus dethroned Vashti and launched a search for the most beautiful young woman in the kingdom to replace her. Enter Esther, the gorgeous Jewish woman whose cousin Mordecai stayed near the royal palace to keep an eye on his young relative.

Haman the Agagite hated Mordecai because he seemed completely unimpressed that the King had promoted Haman and had "set his seat above all the princes who were with him," the Bible says in Esther 3:2. "And all the king's servants who were within the king's gate bowed and paid homage to Haman, for so the king had commanded concerning him. But Mordecai would not bow or pay homage."

Haman was so bitter at Mordecai that he began to plot to kill his nemesis. Consider the power of bitterness. Haman had everything going his way: he was a favourite of King Ahasuerus; he was wealthy; and he had many children. But just the sight of Mordecai banished all the good feelings. Haman couldn't enjoy even a brief moment of his success because of the bitterness and hatred that ruled his heart. His destructive, negative emotions had such a grip on him that they intruded on every situation in his life. They dominated his thought life, his emotions and his entire inner world. Ultimately they destroyed him.

Another Biblical example of bitterness and jealousy is the case of Joseph and his brothers. The other sons of Jacob were bitter against Joseph because he was their father's favourite. (It didn't help that Joseph thought himself better than his brothers and didn't hide it.) They grew to hate Joseph so much that one day, when he came to check up on them, the bitter brothers conspired to murder him.

Unchecked jealousy and bitterness can overcome reason and motivate a person to seek revenge.

King Saul is a classic example of bitterness in the Bible. Saul, Israel's first king, began as a great leader. When David first came to his attention by bravely confronting and killing the Israelite's arch-enemy Goliath, Saul thought, "Hey, this is a great kid!" But as time went on and David gained more and more military victories, and received increasing adulation from the people, Saul became jealous. Perhaps the turning point came when David returned from slaughtering the Philistines. This event is recorded in 1 Samuel 18:6-8. "Now it had happened as they were coming home, when David was returning from the slaughter of the Philistines, that the women had come out of all the cities of Israel, singing and dancing, to meet King Saul with tambourines, with joy, and with musical instruments. So the women sang as they danced and said, 'Saul has slain his thousands, and David his ten thousands.' And Saul was very angry, and the saying displeased him; and he said, 'They have ascribed to David ten thousands and to me they have ascribed only thousands. Now what more can he have but the kingdom?'"

Saul's jealousy of David turned to bitterness, and then to hatred. Saul came to hate David so much he determined to kill him. This can happen when a person doesn't deal with his bitterness. Saul's bitterness was so insidious; he even tried to kill his own son, Jonathan, for defending David.

Bitterness and the other sinful emotions that go with it have deadly consequences. Saul's jealousy and bitterness toward David escalated to the point where he rebelled against God.

Saul had gone to battle against Israel's enemies, the Amalekites, and defeated them—as God had assured him he would. But instead of annihilating every vestige of the enemy, Saul had allowed the Amalekite King Agag to live, and he also loaded up the best plunder. His actions were a blatant contradiction to God's instructions. God could not allow that to go unpunished.

"I greatly regret that I have set up Saul as king, for he has turned back from following Me, and has not performed My commandments" (1 Samuel 15:11). This was God's word to Samuel.

Saul's bitterness and rebellion cost him everything he held dear.

- He lost favour with God.
- He lost his best friend and counselor, Samuel, who said to him, "I will not return with you, for you have rejected the word of the Lord" (1 Samuel 15:26a).
- He lost his kingdom. "The LORD has rejected you from being king over Israel" (1 Samuel 15:26b).
- He lost his three sons. "Then the Philistines followed hard after Saul and his sons. And the Philistines killed Jonathan, Abinadab,

and Malchishua, Saul's sons" (1 Samuel 31:2).

- He lost his own life.
- He lost his entire army. In 1 Samuel 31:6 we read, "So Saul, his three sons, his armor-bearer, and all his men died together that same day." 1 Chronicles 10:13 puts it this way: "So Saul died for his unfaithfulness which he had committed against the LORD, because he did not keep the word of the LORD."

What should King Saul have done? He could have practiced the following spiritual principles that we can use in our own spiritual healing:

- **Nurture a fervent fear of the Lord.** Proverbs 1:7 says, "The fear of the Lord is the beginning of knowledge, but fools despise wisdom and instruction." This fear is a child-like trust in One who is loving, powerful, merciful and always has our best interest in His heart. This fear manifests itself in a passionate desire not to grieve or disappoint our Heavenly Father who never leaves us or forsakes us. We want to spend time with Him, rather than hide from Him. I like the often quoted story where the Sunday school teacher asks her students, "What do you do when Satan comes knocking at your door?"

  "That's easy," said one of the little girls, "I ask Jesus to answer it!" To me, that is a marvelous way to understand the fear and love of God.

- **Desire to have the mind of Christ.** Philippians 2:5-11 advises, "Let this mind be in you which was also in Christ Jesus, who, being in the form of God, did not consider it robbery to be equal with God, but made Himself of no reputation, taking the form of a bondservant, and coming in the likeness of men. And being found in the appearance as a man, He humbled Himself and became obedient to the point of death, even the death of the cross. Therefore God also has highly exalted Him and given Him the name which is above every name, that at the name of Jesus every knee should bow, of those in heaven, and of those on earth and of those under the earth, and that every tongue should confess that Jesus Christ is Lord, to the glory of God the Father."

- **Watch the company we keep.** Ephesians 5:11-15 says, "And have no fellowship with the unfruitful works of darkness, but rather expose them. For it is shameful even to speak of those things which are done by them in secret. But all things that are exposed are made manifest by the light for whatever makes manifest is light. Therefore He says, 'Awake, you who sleep, Arise from the dead. And Christ will give you light.' See then that you walk circumspectly, not as fools but as wise."

- **Be a person of integrity.** Proverbs 20:7: "The righteous man walks in his integrity; his children are blessed after him." A person of integrity is one who can be trusted, is honourable and reliable. It is not what that person says of herself, but the positive affirmation of others of her character. Jesus was a man of integrity.

- **Desire to walk daily in the Holy Spirit and show the fruit of the Spirit in our lives.** The fruit of the Spirit are articulated in Galatians 5: 22, 23 as being "love, joy, peace, long-suffering, kindness, goodness, faithfulness, gentleness, and self-control." Proverbs 22:4 says: "By humility and the fear of the Lord are riches and honor and life."

Remember, there are always consequences to sin and our sin affects many others.

What forgiveness is and what forgiveness is not

There can be no healing from bitterness without forgiveness. Forgiveness sets the stage for healing and creates the environment in which healing can take place. Forgiveness takes away our power to injure ourselves again and again when we remember the wrongs done to us. Forgiveness allows for reconciliation while its opposite, unforgiveness, is the building material of the walls that separate people.

Forgiveness allows us to experience spiritual growth. Achieving forgiveness requires being dependent on the Lord. Forgiveness allows us to build a future and experience genuine intimacy with God, with others, and with ourselves.

Just as it is essential to understand what forgiveness is, it is essential to know what forgiveness is not.

Forgiveness does not mean that we were not hurt or mistreated. It is not feeling that what the other person did to you did not matter when it happened, and that it does not matter now. It does not mean there should be no consequences for the perpetrator. That person still has to be accountable to the Lord and the laws of the land.

Forgiveness is not a feeling that things will get better, that you can pretend everything is settled. It is not the same as reconciliation or restoration of relationship. The person who wronged you must first secure your trust before any of that can take place.

Forgiveness is not the absence of angry feelings. Angry feelings will undoubtedly remain.

How not to sin in your anger

- Focus on God and His forgiveness for you rather than the hurtful statement.
- Express your hurt feelings to God, not others – "God, that personal attack on my character by Leela was hurtful; I just want to get even and lash back at her!"
- Choose to say, "Father I forgive them."
- Refuse to entertain the memory of that hurtful episode.

Forgiveness is not demanding change before you are willing to forgive. It is not bringing up the past, rehashing it, and ranting and raving about the abuse or misuse.

Forgiveness is a beautiful irrationality. It is an undeserved gift that is offered to another. It reflects the highest human virtue. It is surrendering my right to collect an emotional debt from the person who wronged me. It means not seeking payback or revenge. It means not determining to get even.

Corrie ten Boom, whose family offered shelter to persecuted Jewish people during WW II said, "To forgive is to set a prisoner free and realize the prisoner is you."

Forgiveness is both an event (an act of obedience) and an ongoing process. It begins with asking God to forgive us for our own sins and wrongdoings, and then forgiving others.

Jesus taught this lesson to His disciples when they asked Him how they should pray. In the prayer He gave them, known universally as The Lord's Prayer, Jesus told his followers to pray, "...forgive us our sins, as we forgive those who sin against us." If we believe God has forgiven us for all of our sins, how can we not forgive those who have wronged us?

Jesus further reinforced the need for forgiveness with a parable concerning two servants who owed a great debt. In this story in Matthew 18:21-35, Peter had just asked Jesus how many times a person should forgive someone who sinned against him. "Seven times?" Peter wondered.

"No, not seven times," Jesus replied, "but seventy times seven." He went on to tell the story about two servants. The first one owed a tremendous debt to his master, the king—a debt so big there was no hope of him being able to repay it. The servant and his entire family would have to be sold into slavery to pay the debt. But when the servant begged for clemency, the master "was filled with pity for him, and released him and forgave his debt."

What did the forgiven servant do? He went right out and found a fellow servant who owed him a pittance compared to the debt he was forgiven. He grabbed the fellow by the throat and demanded repayment. Immediately. The fellow servant pled with him for mercy. The man would not hear of it. The story goes on to tell how justice came to the first servant when the king heard of his hypocritical actions.

"That," says Jesus, "is what my heavenly Father will do to you if you refuse to forgive your brothers and sisters from your heart."

Because we have been forgiven, we are required to forgive others. That doesn't mean we will necessarily feel like forgiving. We must choose to forgive. We can do this simply by saying, "God, I choose to forgive that person for hurting me."

You may have to make that choice many times, perhaps "seventy times seven" times. But if you will do that, the feeling or desire to forgive will eventually come.

Forgive in the largest increment you can—maybe at first it will only be for thirty seconds at a time, but keep on forgiving.

In forgiving, we let go of the debt. We release the person from owing us anything. This isn't easy, and it isn't something we can do alone. Only with God's help can we accomplish this difficult task.

Sometimes it is easier to feel like forgiving if we begin praying for the person who hurt us, asking God to help us see the person from His perspective. The truth is: hurt people hurt people. The person who hurt you may be a wounded person.

Ask God to bless the person who hurt you. Then bless that person yourself. "Bless those who persecute you; bless and do not curse," says Romans 12:14.

Refuse to live in the past, drowning in self-pity. Trust God and move ahead. Remember that God has promised to bring good from the hurt in your life. We know that because of Romans 8:28 which says, "And we know that all things work together for good to those who love God, to those who are the called according to His purpose." Thank God for that.

Ongoing forgiveness means treating people the way God treats us. God forgives us on an ongoing basis as we confess our sins to Him; including those sins we aren't even aware we've committed.

When I think of the impact of unforgiveness, I always think of the Biblical story of Lazarus in Chapter 11 of John. Lazarus had been dead for four days before Jesus raised him from the dead. When he emerged alive from the tomb, Lazarus was still wrapped in his grave clothes. When I see people imprisoned by their negative emotions, it seems to me they are just like Lazarus—wrapped in filthy grave clothes. Saying to God, "I choose to forgive that person," is like beginning to unwrap the putrid grave wrappings. Saying, "God, I ask You to forgive me, and God, I choose to forgive myself," allows a person to step out of the past and into a life free from the decay of the past. In counseling, I have seen many, many receive freedom as they practiced this.

Ephesians 4:31 and 32 encourages us to "Let all bitterness, wrath, anger, clamour, and evil speaking be put away from you, with all malice. And be kind to one another, tenderhearted, forgiving one another, even as God in Christ forgave you."

Hebrews 12:14,15 says, "Pursue peace with all people, and holiness, without which no one will see the Lord: looking carefully lest anyone fall short of the grace of God; lest any root of bitterness springing up cause trouble, and by this many become defiled...."

Are you bitter? Consider some of the spiritual consequences of bitterness. Reflect on the Bible verses provided.

- Bitterness makes us a prisoner. Remember King Saul's bitterness.
- Bitterness robs us of God's blessing. 1 Peter 3:8, 9
- Bitterness causes us to lose the sense of God's presence and power within us. Ephesians 3:20; 2 Corinthians 4:17; James 3:14-18
- Bitterness causes physical, emotional and mental problems. Proverbs 11:17; Psalm 32; Psalm 51
- Bitterness brings unforgiveness from God. Matthew 6:12-15; Matthew 5:7; Matthew 18: 23-25
- Bitterness gives Satan an advantage and a foothold in your life. 2 Corinthians 2:10, 11; Ephesians 4:22-27
- Bitterness brings with it the judgement of God. James 5:19; Matthew 18:28-35
- Bitterness impacts all those around us, because bitterness and unforgiveness motivate us to get even and hurt others. Ecclesiastes 9:18b; Proverbs 27:17

If you are bitter, do not despair. Remember these spiritual attitudes and disciplines that can empower you to live a healthy life:
- Forgive those who have hurt you.
- Have a fervent fear of God.
- Desire to have the mind of Christ.
- Watch the company you keep.
- Be a person of integrity.
- Desire to walk daily in the Holy Spirit and show the fruits of the Spirit in your life.
- Ask someone to help you be accountable for forgiveness.

Remember, God never asks us to do anything He will not help us do. He promises to provide the strength we need. "I can do all things through Christ who strengthens me" (Philippians 4: 13).

Prayer:

"Lord, Your Word says, 'In returning and rest you shall be saved; in quietness and confidence shall be your strength' (Isaiah 30:15). Neither rest, nor quietness, nor confidence exists in my life right now. I'm so caught up in pain it consumes me. Please shine Your light into my dark places so I can be free of the unforgiveness that plagues my heart. Your Word also tells me that I am to bless You at all times for You offer great benefits to those who trust in You. You graciously extend the forgiveness of all my sins and the healing of all my diseases (Psalm 103:2-3). I know I need that benefit package in my life. I accept Your forgiveness and healing; by an act of faith I forgive those who have hurt me, letting go of the raging thoughts that have preoccupied and overwhelmed me. In Jesus' name."

Chapter 6: Anger:
The Volcano Within

A headline in the newspaper of a major Canadian city caught my attention: "Angry driver rams crowd; 2 dead, 2 hurt." The account began: "A car plowed through a line-up at a bus stop Monday, leaving two dead and two young girls seriously injured. A 22-year-old man was to appear in court today to face two counts of murder and two of attempted murder. The incident began Monday morning as crowds streamed from a park...following a local celebration featuring fireworks. An argument started after a car stopped for a red light. The driver became upset when his woman passenger talked to.... standing in the line-up at the bus stop near a subway station."

The article goes on to describe how the driver made a U-turn and drove his car into the crowd at the bus stop, killing the man and an 18-year-old woman.

Now, that's anger. More accurately, it is rage that's gone way out-of-control.

What is anger?
Unger's Bible Dictionary defines anger as: "The emotion of instant displeasure and indignation arising from the feeling of injury done or intended, or from the discovery of offense against law" (Moody Press of Chicago, 1988).

Anger is an emotional response to circumstances. It is a feeling, but one with strong ties to our thinking and clear connections to the physical. Anger is a gnawing sense of inner turmoil, a response to some frustration that has persisted for a long period of time.

Anger can stem from a variety of other emotional stimuli. One Sunday afternoon when our son was small, he and a neighbour boy were playing outside. Because we were heading to church soon, I went to call him for supper.

He didn't answer and he didn't come.

This was exactly the time a sexual predator was loose in the city. I panicked. I alerted the neighbours and over the next hour we drove the streets, hollering the boys' names. With each passing moment we became more convinced that our boys had been abducted. When fear takes over, the mind can travel in unpredictable directions.

Sick with dread and desperation, I hauled out my bike and began pedaling down the alley. I hadn't gotten very far before I heard a little voice call, "Hi, Daddy!"

My fear morphed into blazing anger. While I was unspeakably happy and relieved to find my son, anger at the anxiety he had caused us consumed me. I'm not proud of the way I acted with him that day. It was not his fault that I let circumstances and fear blow my emotions way out of proportion and culminate in an explosion of anger. It was not my usual approach to yell at my children, so when my son heard this from me, he was so frightened he fell off the bike he had been innocently riding around the neighbourhood.

Angry words can wound, damage and destroy. Anger can ruin relationships. Anger can also motivate a person to hate. Proverbs 16:32 says: "He who is slow to anger is better than the mighty, and he who rules his spirit than he who takes a city."

There are three words for anger in Greek: *orge, thumos,* and *parogismos. Orge* refers to a settled or abiding, slow-rising condition of the mind that seeks revenge. It says, "One day you will pay for hurting me. I'll get even." A good Biblical picture of *orge* would be Joseph's brothers, whose resentment and anger toward their younger brother rose to the point of wanting to kill him. *Thumos,* or wrath, is an agitated condition, an outburst from the indignation within that blazes up quickly and disappears. It's what happens when someone cuts you off in traffic. As a high school teacher, I observed that one of the favourite pranks of my student, Jeremy, was to come up behind a fellow student and pull the books out of his arms. It was obvious that the other students did not appreciate this. Usually by the time the books were picked up and the laughing stopped, the anger had dissipated.

Parogismos is the energy we experience when an obstacle hinders the fulfillment of our need. This kind of anger carries the idea of righteous resentment or provocation, the feeling that "I have a right to be angry because of what has happened." Luke, the assistant pastor believed he would move into the senior pastor's role when the senior pastor left. That did not happen. The church board decided to call another pastor for the position. Instead of accepting the board's decision, Luke resigned in anger that very Sunday. I believe he lost a lot of respect from many people. Jim is another example. He knew he was the better football player, but Coach chose the son of a friend for the team instead of him. Therefore, Jim felt justified in expressing anger.

These same levels of anger could be described as indignation, resentment, and rage. They are vigorous expressions that combine emotion, physical response, cognition, and behaviour. In other words, when we are swept up in any one of these expressions, we are totally involved.

Rage is a visible expression of uncontrolled anger. Resentment is a repressed feeling of anger that smoulders and seeks revenge. With this type of anger, we are forced by societal pressures to resolve our rage in an unhealthy way. For many people, the common pattern is to deny the existence of angry feelings and push them down inside. This inevitably leads to tension and subtle attacks on others.

The Root Causes of Anger

Dr. Dwight Carlson offers a personal illustration of how hurt and anger are so closely tied together. I have encouraged many of my clients to read his book and apply the principles.

Carlson tells of his 13-year-old son walking by him and calling him Chubby, not Dad. His son's words dug deep. Carlson admits the negative statement led to anger. The good thing that happened as a result was a chubby dad worked hard and lost 20 pounds.

Anger is learned. If we are angry, short-tempered people, we have likely spent time with people who were or are the same, and we've learned to be like them.

Anger can spring from selfishness. The more a person becomes absorbed with himself, the greater his needs appear to be. Wanting them fulfilled in his own way often stems from a sense of inferiority. "Do not hasten in your spirit to be angry, for anger rests in the bosom of fools" (Ecclesiastes 7:9).

Anger can come from blocked goals. When you have a goal that is either temporarily or permanently out of reach, it is normal to feel angry. If a person or a circumstance becomes a barrier to attaining that goal, our response may be anger. The barrier may be a minor disappointment (having someone break into the grocery store line-up in front of you), or a significant loss or disappointment. Perhaps you plan to go on a trip and something happens to prevent you: the car breaks down or the money isn't available. An incapacitating illness ends your career. Another person dreams of a specific career but is unable to achieve that dream. These are all blocked goals that might generate anger.

Anger comes from violation of our rights. And what do we believe our rights are?

- to be loved, consoled, secure
- to be accepted as an individual
- to be treated fairly
- to be allowed to express personal opinions
- to be able to achieve a particular goal.

Planning our own free time, earning and spending our own money, choosing our own friends, and controlling our personal belongings might also be considered personal rights. Privacy is another right. Having mom or dad always checking the kids' rooms to see if they're bringing home certain forbidden things does not allow for the privacy a young person needs.

Anger comes from righteous reasons. This is a sense of deep indignation over the reality gap between what is and what ought to be. Idealistic thinkers have difficulty accepting the reality of injustice and the slowness of change. The positive solution is to deal with your idealism and channel your anger in a constructive way to influence what changes are possible. A friend of mine who works in the justice system travelled to an Asian country. He outraged over the corruption and injustice he witnessed there. His response was to become involved in an international justice initiative that functions in that country. A woman who spent her life as a missionary in Cambodia decided to retire in that country and establish a home for children orphaned by AIDS. She was angered by the high incidence of child prostitution in that country, and became actively involved in a rescue initiative.

Derogatory remarks and put-downs can also cause anger. We may be called names like stupid or dumb. Having someone say we'll never amount to anything can also give rise to anger, particularly if the remarks are taken to heart and rolled out of proportion. Carlson's story of his son calling him 'Chubby' is a good example here.

Sam was a medical doctor and a client of mine. He needed help dealing with his self-image and his anger toward his father. From the time he was a child, Sam's father had told him he was stupid, that he would never amount to anything. Sam worked desperately to prove his father wrong, and upon receiving his medical diploma, he phoned his father and said: "Dad, I am now a medical doctor."

"So what?" his father said. "You're still stupid."

My work as a counselor was to empower Sam to forgive his father and work on his personal need fulfillment. His need was not actually for acceptance from his father. His need was for a relationship with Christ apart from his dad. He needed to recognize that Christ accepted him as a person of worth. I encouraged Sam to pray against Satan's attacks this way: "In the name of Jesus Christ, I rebuke the lies of my dad."

I brought Sam's attention to Psalm 139:13-18: "For you formed my inward parts; You covered me in my mother's womb. I will praise You, for I am fearfully and wonderfully made. Marvellous are Your works, and that my soul knows very well. My frame was not hidden from You when I was made in secret, and skilfully wrought in the lowest parts of the earth. Your eyes saw my substance, being yet unformed. And in Your book they all were written, the days fashioned for me when as yet there were none of them. How precious also are Your thoughts to me, Oh God! How great is the sum of them! If I should count them, they would be more in number than the sand; When I awake, I am still with You."

Romans 8:37-39 also helped Sam. It says: "Yet in all these things, we are more than conquerors through Him who loved us. For I am persuaded that neither death nor life, nor angels nor principalities nor powers, nor things present nor things to come, nor height nor depth, nor any other created thing, shall be able to separate us from the love of God which is in Christ Jesus our Lord."

Often, people don't like to own up to anger. They will use all sorts of euphemisms to describe their feelings. No one likes to admit to bitterness, intolerance or hatred, unforgiveness, malice, wrath, gossip, revenge, or jealousy.

On the other hand, how often do we freely acknowledge feeling miffed, hurt, irked, annoyed, absolutely furious, cranky, touchy, disgruntled, huffy, spiteful, crushed, or ticked off?

How Is Anger Manifested?

Unresolved anger can generate physical responses in the body, such as increased heart rate, or an unusual rush of energy.

Mild anger causes one to feel cross, peeved, annoyed, or irritated. That is fairly normal. Your garden is looking lovely and then a soccer ball veers off course and crushes your favourite rose bush. A student walking in the hallway gets his hat knocked off or his books flicked out from under his arm.

Moderate anger reveals itself when we are aggravated, frustrated, provoked, disgusted, hurt, or offended. It seemed that Vic had the worst of luck when it came to cars. The dealer assured him that the car, even though a used vehicle, was in good shape. Over the months to follow, Vic was feeling used and abused because of the bills he was paying to keep his car in good working order. He grew disgusted with the salesman who sold him the car, frustrated with the car dealership and was ready to go public because of the offence.

Explosions, fury, and rage characterize intense anger. There are physical changes: trembling or shaking; twitching in the face; the neck and/or shoulders lock up. There may be pressure in the head and a lump in the throat, over-secreting saliva glands or dry mouth, shallow breathing or a racing or pounding heart.

The individual with intense anger may be consumed by repetitive thoughts relating to people or events that have caused their pain or disappointment. They experience feelings of bitterness, alienation, loneliness or self-pity. Thoughts of revenge or harming themselves may arise. Intense anger can result in actions that are dismissive of others or withdrawing from others on the one hand, and violent, vindictive and cruel on the other. 2 Samuel 18:14 shares the cruelty of Joab, who murdered the helpless Absalom even though King David said to protect his son.

Anger may also be disguised. Six common ways of disguising anger are suggested by Carlson in his book *Overcoming Hurts and Anger* (used with permission). In my years of counseling, I have seen these six categories show up in my office again and again. I have come up with my own terms for some of Carlson's categories.

1. The Passive/Aggressive Person. This individual is characterized by aggressive behaviour exhibited in passive ways such as pouting, stubbornness, and procrastination. He often takes the opposite point of view or opposes others' actions. He is Mr. Contradictory. If you say things are black, he will say they're white. Prolonged contact with this type of person can be extremely frustrating. Marriages are destroyed by a spouse who operates this way. Many partners have said to me, "If it weren't for the kids, I'd be gone."

2. The List-Keeper. This person is also known as a martyr or a collector of injustices. She is the one who carefully saves up each little grievance, annoyance, or irritation. She tells herself that each grievance is not enough in itself to deal with, but she never forgets it. After she has taken enough abuse, she becomes outraged.

3. The Retreater. This person suddenly retreats into an icy silence when something is bothering him. When you ask if anything is wrong, he flatly denies it, but still manages to let everyone know he's upset by making terse, grumpy remarks. We have plenty of 'Retreaters' in our churches—people who sit scowling, with crossed arms, not saying a word. But their disapproval over the sermon, or the way the deacons are handling things, or the music the worship team has chosen, is patently obvious.

4. The Mask of Sweetness. This person is always super-sweet and yet it is apparent there is something inside she is covering up. I think of the pastor's wife who had to listen to negative comments about her husband, yet remains sweet in order to protect the ministry. Inside, she was seething with anger and found herself avoiding a particular congregation member who was making the hurtful statements. The only way for her to deal with her anger was to say, "God, I choose to forgive that person," and to pray specifically for him.

5. Mr. Negativity. This individual is critical, often sarcastic, about everything. His criticisms are generally supported by seemingly well-founded rational or intellectual reasoning, but through it all one can sense an undertone of anger, hostility, and negativism.

6. The 'It's my fault' Individual. This person will shoulder the blame for anything; even things for which he is in no way responsible. He is self-effacing and never appears to be angry, but the peaceful aura is a sham.

How Does *Your* Anger Manifest Itself?
Anger is a very versatile emotion. It may be actively displayed in hitting, punching, throwing objects, slamming doors, yelling and swearing. On the other hand, silence, resentment, irritability and bitter hatred are the more subtle symptoms of intense, suppressed anger.

Can you see yourself in any of Dr. Carlson's categories? Does your anger manifest itself in any of the following ways?
- Blowing up – the volcano approach. Sometimes you see this at the church general meeting when an issue comes to a vote and a disgruntled member stomps out to express his anger at the outcome.
- Blaming others – "It's not *my* fault...if *he* hadn't done what he did, I wouldn't be angry."

- Silence, pouting, and withdrawal – collecting all your hurts and disappointments and then saying, "I don't want to talk about it." Or maybe it is daydreaming (escaping into the mind and replaying the hurts and angers); suicidal thoughts and tendencies; escaping into drugs and/or alcohol.
- Rebellion, getting even – consciously or unconsciously doing what others dislike; often disguised as chronic forgetfulness, boredom, correcting and interrupting, sexual teasing, or open revenge.
- Arguing and nagging – being contrary to everything that is said in the discussion; keeping track of past wrongs accurately and precisely, being sure to bring them up whenever possible.

Dr. Tim LaHaye and author Bob Phillips developed an Irritability Quotient rating scale on the emotion of anger, in their excellent book *Anger is a Choice*. This exhaustive survey is worth checking out, to determine your own potential areas of growth in dealing with anger in a spiritually healthy way. Most Christian bookstores would offer this popular book, or you can also easily order it online.

Effects of prolonged anger

Medical studies have shown that over time, prolonged anger can have a detrimental impact on a person's physical well-being. Psychological studies reveal that anger affects romance, work, parenting, and social relationships. In families, angry attitudes and beliefs can move between and beyond generations. As I reflect on my own experiences in the foster home, I can't help wondering if my foster mother had those sorts of issues herself.

The impact of familial anger was graphically driven home in the example of twin boys who were constantly angry with each other, always in each other's face. They were fiercely competitive, continually fighting. Their anger culminated one day when one grabbed a butcher knife and stabbed his twin brother in the chest and killed him.

King Solomon reminds us in Proverbs 29:22 that "An angry man stirs up strife, and a furious man abounds in transgression."

Late one night, I received a phone call from a woman who was literally holding a knife in front of her to protect herself from her abusive husband. In situations like this, when we eventually sit down to talk, it is not uncommon to learn that abuse in their own life has caused the anger in the abusive partner. They are lashing out because of their own experience.

I went to the couple's home to talk with them. These were two Bible college students; both had made commitments to Christ. The wife came from the background of an abusive father; the husband was a young Christian who lacked spiritual maturity. I advised them that Satan, not God, was in control of their home and their relationship. I had them kneel together and ask God to forgive them. Then, they asked forgiveness from each other.

During my years as a classroom teacher I came to realize that students who acted in anger were not necessarily angry with me. There were also some students who were being pressured and negatively impacted by someone else's anger. I think of one student, the daughter of a scientist. Rachel was an excellent student, but when her father came to parent-teacher interviews, he was extremely upset. He felt his daughter should have received more than 90% in my English class. I explained in detail how I arrived at the score. I stressed that it was a very good mark. He was not satisfied. After he left, I recalled many times when Rachel had come to me during the year to say, "Mr. Pringle would you please read my paper again? I think I did better than this mark." Having to deal with her father's anger caused a great deal of fear and anxiety for Rachel. The father was an angry man. There wasn't anything his daughter could do about it. He was giving her the impression that she would only be good enough for him if she achieved higher marks. I did my best to communicate to the father what he was doing to his daughter, but he wouldn't listen.

What Does The Bible Say About Anger?
The Bible offers several character studies of angry people. King Saul's anger, fuelled by insecurity and fear, prompted him to try to kill David. Saul could have been helped if he would have had Hebrews 12:14, 15 to apply to his life. We are reminded in those verses not to allow any root of bitterness to control us, because bitterness is destructive and defiles many people.

Out of anger and jealousy, Cain killed his brother Abel. Moses had repeated bouts of anger over the disobedience of the Hebrew people. His classic exhibition of anger was when he disobeyed God's specific direction to touch the rock to release God's miracle of producing life-sustaining water. Instead, Moses struck it in anger. The consequence of his action was that he was not allowed to enter the Promised Land.

The Apostle James advises readers to deal with anger by being "… swift to hear, slow to speak, slow to wrath; for the wrath of man does not produce the righteousness of God" (James 1:19).

Nabal, described in 1 Samuel 25, was a very angry man who refused David and his men food, even though his flocks and workers had been under David's protection. When David vowed vengeance, only the good sense and diplomacy of Nabal's wife Abigail spared his life.

Jonah was angry when God asked him to go to Nineveh to warn the citizens of coming judgement. Jonah hated the Assyrian Ninevites and had no desire to spare them from the punishment he felt they rightfully deserved for their sin and abuse of the Israelite people. He was angry that God would even consider giving the Ninevites an opportunity to repent. Those Biblical examples show that anger is normal. What matters is what we do with it.

Things You Need To Know About Your Anger

Anger is a choice. People and world events do not make you angry; you choose to be angry. Even when a genuinely negative event occurs, it is the meaning you attach to it that determines your emotional response. The fact that you are responsible for your anger is an advantage, because it gives you the opportunity to achieve control and make a free choice about how you want to feel.

Your loss of self-worth can make you angry. When people criticize you, disagree with you, or fail to behave as you want them to, a great deal of the anger you feel comes as defence against your loss of self-worth. Such anger is self-defeating; what causes you to lose self-esteem is your own negatively distorted thoughts.

Most of the time your anger will not help you. Instead, anger and hostility can immobilize you. More often than not, the thoughts that generate anger will contain distortions, and correcting these distortions will reduce your anger. For example, anger over childhood issues will worsen and become exaggerated if not dealt with. To do so, call anger what it is: a spiritual stronghold. Ask God to help you pull down the strongholds of anger.

The Bible speaks of strongholds and how to deal with them this way: "For the weapons of our warfare are not carnal but mighty in God for pulling down strongholds, casting down arguments and every high thing that exalts itself against the knowledge of God, bringing every thought into captivity to the obedience of Christ" (2 Corinthians 10:3-5).

Others may not see your anger as legitimate. If you can try to look at the world through other peoples' eyes, you may be surprised to discover that from their point of view, their actions are not unfair. Some of your resentment and frustration may vanish if you are able to let go of the notion that your concepts of truth, justice and fairness are shared by everyone. Proverbs 19:11 explains that "the discretion of a man makes him slow to anger, and his glory is to overlook a transgression."

Anger does not achieve your goals. Anger is unlikely to help you achieve *any* positive goals in your dealings with people. In fact, your rage will often cause further polarization and deterioration of the situation. Even if you do get what you want, any short-term gains will likely be offset by long-term resentment and retaliation. For example, you're a cashier at the grocery store, seething with anger over criticism from a parent, spouse, or possibly a fellow-employee, and you vent your anger on a customer who is taking too long to count out the exact change. You may experience some short-term satisfaction in letting your anger out, but in the long-run, that behaviour will have far-reaching consequences for you and your job, because no one likes to be embarrassed or intimidated.

Anger can stem from unrealistic expectations. Frustration may lead to anger, which may come from unrealistic expectations or beliefs. Examples of unrealistic expectations might be: "If I want something, I deserve it." "If I work hard at something, I should be successful."

"Other people should measure up to my standards." "I should be able to solve my problems quickly and easily."

The Biblical teaching of trusting God rather than ourselves presents a whole new perspective on the matter. Proverbs 3:5, 6 says: "Trust in the Lord with all your heart and lean not on your own understanding; in all your ways acknowledge Him and He shall direct your paths."

Remember, we need to realize that we are responsible for our anger. Anger is a choice. People don't make us angry; we choose to be angry.

Anger Is Not Sinful In Itself, But It Can Lead To Sin

Anger is not evil. If it were, could a perfect God be angry? The Bible speaks often of God's anger. Jesus was angry with the money-changers who desecrated the holy temple. There is such a thing as holy or righteous anger, but anger that is not righteous can lead to sin. Paul instructed Ephesian Christians not to "… let the sun go down on your wrath, nor give place to the devil" (Ephesians 4:26, 27).

Anger is sinful when it rises too soon, without deflection, and when the expression and intensity of the anger does not equal the injury that awakens it. When we lash out at others in anger, it is definitely sinful.

How To Deal With An Angry Person

If you live with or interact with an angry person, the way you speak and act toward that person may need to be modified. First, question whether or not you are responsible for causing their anger. If the answer is yes, then apologize and do whatever is possible to restore relations.

Avoid the delay tactic where you say, "If you want to talk about this, we can, but not while you're so upset and unreasonable. You aren't even talking sense right now. Once you settle down and act civilized, then we'll talk." This approach makes the relationship conditional and the other person even more angry. It does not accept the person as worthwhile. Do not try to appear oblivious, maintaining a blank, disinterested expression and ignoring the other person's anger. This says, "You don't exist," and is the most emotionally devastating response possible. Avoid speaking with an "I'm smart/you're stupid" tone of voice. This only prompts competitive argument. Do not indulge in as much screaming, jumping, and combative physical gestures as the angry person. Don't play amateur psychologist.

Now that we've cleared away what *not* to do, here is a road map for dealing with someone caught in the grip of anger.

First, demonstrate acceptance of the individual as a person and show a willingness to understand the issues and causes of their anger. Show acceptance by speaking slowly, keeping your body relaxed and avoiding dramatic gestures. Move slowly. Use direct and steady eye contact. Let the person talk. Treat them with respect and cooperation, acceptance and dignity. Remember, anger is usually a secondary emotion and there is probably underlying pain.

Work to create a calm dialogue to help you both understand the angry person's feelings and the cause of his anger. Involve the appropriate person or persons qualified to take constructive action. This may mean calling a social worker, a counselor or a pastor to help.

If You Are The Angry Person

Two things are important to remember when you're angry. First, recognize your vulnerability to becoming angry. Admit, "I am an angry person and I need to guard against it." Secondly, accept that uncontrolled anger leads to bitterness, hatred, and even violence. Anger can be released in a creative and constructive way. Recognize and accept your anger. When the emotion hits, admit it: "I am angry."

When I present marriage seminars, I often point out that half of the audience members probably have a tendency to be an angry person, and the other half tend to be fearful, just because of their innate characteristics, personalities and temperaments. What takes us overboard in situations is the circumstances. The angry person will attack; the fearful person will retreat further and further.

I have a tendency to react to provocation with anger, whereas my younger brother is more likely to become fearful. When we were teenagers in the foster home and our foster mother locked us out of the house, my brother didn't want to make any waves. He wanted to let it go. I, on the other hand, wanted to kick the door down. When I became a follower of Christ and would experience anger, I would say, "God, I am angry and I know unchecked anger is sinful, so I repent of it." Consider what 1 John 1:9 says, "If we confess our sins, He is faithful and just to forgive us our sins and to cleanse us from all unrighteousness."

People often feel they get personal benefits from being angry. They enjoy the emotional high and the sense of control it gives them.

Consider the short-term and long-term consequences of anger to see if the benefits are really worth it. Recognize the cause of your anger. Is your anger legitimate? Ask yourself why you are angry. Perhaps, as a child, you were not allowed to express anger to your parents or authority figures. A person coming from that experience may be inclined to display anger to employees, just because you are now the boss and in control. Many of the abused women I counsel experience such intense anger that they routinely lash out at people. In some cases, the anger has been pushed deep down inside and comes out in other ways, as eating disorders, or some type of illness. Anyone or anything that crosses us up means another blocked goal. If we're told, "no" when we want a "yes," that's a blocked goal, and a blocked goal can make us angry.

Identify the source of your anger. In order to determine that, it might be helpful to keep an anger journal where you note each time you get angry. Include any instances of moderate or intense anger. Give the reason. Some examples may have more than one cause. A common source of anger is an attack on your self-esteem. Remember the woman from a previous chapter who had trouble grasping mathematics as a schoolgirl? She would be sick with nerves when the teacher sent her to the board to solve a problem in front of the whole class. When she failed to get the correct answer, the teacher would say to the class, "Clap for her. She's so stupid." Georgia said to me, "Thirty years later, I still remember that teacher's name and I still hate her." I challenged Georgia to work on forgiving the teacher, and praying for freedom from the painful memories.

Hurtful comments or statements can make us extremely angry: "You're a loser...you're stupid...no one will want to marry you...you'll never get a job...you're too fat...you're too lazy...too ugly." All of this gets programmed into a person's mind. Soon we begin to believe it is true.

Outright criticism or abuse is easy to identify, but if someone tries to dominate you, or walks away when you are still talking to her, she is effectively saying, "My wishes and needs are more important than yours. You don't matter."

In my own childhood, many things made me angry, including the fact that whenever something was stolen in the community, people immediately assumed the Pringle boys were responsible. They often said derogatory things about us and called us ugly names which sharpened and deepened my anger.

It is important to replace derogatory and deprecating self-talk with statements that affirm truth. Remind yourself that God made you in His image.

"Then God said, 'Let Us make man in Our image, according to Our likeness; let them have dominion over the fish of the sea, over the birds of the air, and over the cattle, over all the earth and over every creeping thing that creeps on the earth.' So God created man in His own image; in the image of God He created him; male and female He created them" (Genesis 1: 26, 27).

Determine a possible course of action for your anger. Displacing your anger is not an option. If, in response to a surge of anger, you walk outside and kick the first thing you see—the cat perhaps, you know intuitively this is not an appropriate response. The cat didn't do anything. The problem is yours. You need to acknowledge that.

An employee angry with his boss may be tempted to erupt at home with totally innocent family members, or he may fall into cold silence. Neither is appropriate.

Sometimes our instinctive actions represent a lack of self-control. What's behind that lack of control? Did you ever get to voice your hurts and pain as a child? Maybe you gave the teacher grief in school, but the teacher wasn't the problem. It was your mom and dad divorcing and your dad saying to your mom, "I never want to see you again." Or maybe, because you were a kid, you were never allowed to argue your case against unfair parental treatment, and you took out your frustration on your teacher.

When dealing with a spouse or other close family member on a one-to-one basis, express your angry feelings clearly. Say, "I feel rejected when you yell and scream at me," instead of, "You make me angry!" Convey the primary feelings; anger is usually a secondary feeling or a reaction to some insult, threat, put-down, or frustration. Rather than saying to a son or daughter, "You are really stupid," try, "It really bothers me that you are sloughing off when I know you have the ability to do better in school..."

Never say, "You never..." or "You always..." On the other hand, don't manipulate with, "It's my entire fault..." when you don't really mean it.

Compromise when appropriate. This is an integral characteristic of the emotionally and mentally mature individual. Be humble: after all, you could be wrong!

Choose to stop anger. Anger that stays with us becomes resentment and bitterness. Stopping anger is a choice—not an easy one, but definitely a do-able one.

Give up your desire to strike back.

In his letter to the Romans, the Apostle Paul says, "Repay no one evil for evil. Have regard for good things in the sight of all men. If it is possible, as much as depends on you, live peaceably with all men. Beloved, do not avenge yourselves, but rather give place to wrath; for it is written, 'Vengeance is Mine, I will repay,' says the Lord. Therefore, 'If your enemy is hungry, feed him; If he is thirsty, give him drink; For in so doing you will heap coals of fire on his head.' Do not be overcome with evil, but overcome evil with good" (Romans 12:17-21).

If we know a certain person makes us angry whenever we encounter him, we need to be praying for that person ahead of time so the behaviour will stop.

Is there a certain situation that regularly creates anger in you? Call it what it is and either avoid the situation or "get prayed-up" ahead of time.

Actively search for a creative solution to your anger. What can you do to correct the difficulty, or at least reduce the chance you'll be hurt in the same way in the future? If there is no solution, because the situation is totally out of your control, you will only make yourself miserable with your resentment, so why not get rid of it? This requires help from God's Word, and diligent prayer.

Delay anger by working to control your thoughts. In order to behave and talk in a positive way, analyze the thoughts that automatically come when you begin to get angry. Make a list of your behaviours ("The last time I was with that person, this is how I behaved... thought...acted toward them.") Recognize the behaviours that are wrong. Make a list of your angry responses. Plan ahead by writing down positive statements to replace the things you usually say. Sometimes we get angry with people we don't even know. Consider writing down possible explanations for such anger. ("Am I angry at that person because she has more money? A better car? He stole my girlfriend?")

Remember that mind-reading is not a legitimate response when you are imagining other people's motives. This occurs often in marriages. You think you know what your spouse is thinking, but that isn't necessarily so.

Control your actions. To avoid an angry outburst, refrain from taking any action until the situation is thought through and you are in control. To gain control and deal properly with your anger, it may be necessary to use one or more first-aid strategies for calming down or cooling off. Divert your attention with calming activities, listening to inspirational music and trying to maintain positive thoughts.

Key to spiritual healing is remembering that positive thoughts come from God's Word.

"Blessed is the man who walks not in the counsel of the ungodly, nor stands in the path of sinners, nor sits in the seat of the scornful. But his delight is in the law of the Lord, and in His law he meditates day and night. He shall be like a tree planted by the rivers of water, that brings forth its fruit in its season, whose leaf also shall not wither; and whatever he does shall prosper" (Psalm 1:1-3).

"For the word of God is living and powerful, and sharper than any two-edged sword, piercing even to the division of the soul and spirit, and of joints and marrow, and is a discerner of the thoughts and intents of the heart. And there is no creature hidden from His sight, but all things are naked and open to the eyes of Him to whom we must give account. Seeing that we have a great High Priest who has passed through the heavens, Jesus the Son of God, let us hold fast our confession. For we do not have a High Priest who cannot sympathize with our weaknesses, but was in all points tempted as we are, yet without sin. Let us therefore come boldly to the throne of grace, that we may obtain mercy and find grace to help in time of need" (Hebrews 4:12-16).

"Let this mind be in you which was also in Christ Jesus, who being in the form of God, did not consider it robbery to be equal with God, but made Himself of no reputation, taking the form of a bondservant, and coming in the likeness of men. And being found in appearance as a man, He humbled Himself and became obedient to the point of death, even the death of the cross. Therefore God also has highly exalted Him and given Him the name which is above every name, that at the name of Jesus every knee should bow, of those in heaven, and of those on earth, and of those under the earth, and that every tongue shall confess that Jesus Christ is Lord, to the glory of God the Father" (Philippians 2:5-11).

More Practical Solutions to Anger

- Channel your anger energy into something positive like physical exercise (walking, jogging) or some manual activity.
- Do something helpful for someone else. Do you have a neighbour or friend who might need your help for a small task?
- Talk with a trusted friend.
- Write it down. In counseling clients, I often encourage them to journal. It can be a very strategic way to diminish intense emotions.
- Review your self-talk often during the day. Literally set a clock and check at regular intervals to see how you've done. At the very least, make sure you do this at the end of each day. It is also helpful to have someone trustworthy keeping you accountable.
- Choose to give God your angry thoughts. An appropriate prayer might be, "God, I choose to meditate on Your Word rather than let angry thoughts control me." This is a choice. Memorize scripture verses and repeat them to yourself whenever anger threatens. Write the verses on 3" x 5" cards and carry them in your purse or shirt pocket, or post them on the refrigerator door or the bathroom mirror for instant review whenever anger rises.
- Pray about your anger. One might pray this way: "Lord, I've been hurt by people and events, and as a result, anger has been a part of me for a while now. I've felt entitled to it because of what I've endured. Yet more and more, I am seeing anger as a vicious taskmaster that doesn't allow me any freedom or peace. I am torn. I despise my anger because it keeps me from building genuine relationships and developing my God-given potential. On the other hand, I love my anger because it keeps ME in control.

But Your Word, in James 1:20 says, 'Everyone should be quick to listen, slow to speak and slow to become angry, for man's anger does not bring about the righteous life that God desires.' I see how true that is, because I'm so consumed with anger I can't possibly understand Your heart for my life. Lord, please replace my anger with a righteous life like Your Word says. I know that's what I need; I just can't do it on my own.

Some days I'm sure I'm finished with anger, with leaving behind the memories and agonies, but like the chime of a clock, those thoughts and feelings return with regularity, crushing my resolve to be free. God, I need help! You're the only one who can restore me. Please don't let me stay in this place of hostility and rage. It's wearing me down and I want to be free.

In John 8:34-36, You say, 'I tell you the truth, everyone who sins is a slave to sin. Now, a slave has no permanent place in the family, but a son belongs to it forever. So if the Son [Jesus] sets you free, you are free indeed.' Lord Jesus, I am in that place where I need freedom. I don't want to be a slave; I want to live and be a fully functioning part of Your family. Please set me free from anger and all the accompanying thoughts and emotions that have plagued me. Give me the courage to embrace all You have for me. In the name of Jesus, Amen."

- Choose to forgive. Forgiveness is a choice. You may not feel like forgiving, but if you make the choice to forgive, and tell God about your decision, saying, "God, I choose to forgive," your feelings will eventually catch up. Keep repeating the process until that happens.

In my many years of experience, I have found that a person cannot deal effectively with anger if he does not know Jesus Christ personally. To know Him, you must sincerely repent of your sin of anger, ask Jesus to forgive you, and invite Him to come in and control your life.

How to Get Started With Jesus Christ

If you have not committed your life to a relationship with Jesus, that is the first step in seeking spiritual healing.

- Read the book of Mark in the Bible. If you don't have a Bible, call a local church and ask for one, or visit a local Christian bookstore and ask them for a recommendation.
- Call a pastor or good Christian friend and share your desire to enter into a relationship with Jesus.
- Start attending a local, Biblically-based church right away. Commit to being in fellowship with other Christians on a regular basis.

Chapter 7: I'm out of Control: Obsessive-Compulsive Behaviours

"Stella, Stella, Stella...you've locked that door at least twenty-seven times tonight. Every night we go through this same routine. You go to the door. You check it. You lock it. You unlock it. You lock it again. Five minutes later, you're back checking it, locking it, unlocking it and locking it again. You're driving me crazy with your obsessive behaviour." By the time Stella and her husband came to my office for help, Roger almost wanted to divorce Stella. He couldn't stand the bizarre, repetitive, obsessive-compulsive ritual she went through every night.

It didn't take long to discover that Stella had a reason for checking and rechecking the locks. Many years before, a burglar had broken into their home. This created a deep insecurity in Stella. After that trauma, she made very sure she locked and double-locked the door. Now, twenty years later, she was still doing it. Locking the door had become an obsession, a compulsion blown way out of proportion.

What Is Obsessive-Compulsive Behaviour?

An obsessive-compulsive reaction is characterized by disturbing, unwanted, anxiety-provoking, intruding thoughts or ideas, and repetitive impulses to perform certain acts such as drinking, counting, checking, hoarding, and hand-washing.

To the individual controlled by the compulsive-obsessive behaviour, the act itself is distasteful, undesirable and abnormal. For those whose lives are connected to the obsessive individual, the behaviour is baffling and often disgusting. For instance, I have worked with women who literally pull out their hair—one hair at a time.

Tim was a hoarder. He had a compulsion to save cigarette packages—not just his own, but any he found on the street or in garbage cans. Whenever he found an empty cigarette package, Tim would bring it home and stash it in his closet. The space was now stuffed with thousands and thousands of dirty, used cigarette packages. It was driving his parents crazy.

What Causes Obsessive-Compulsive Behaviour?

Obsessive-compulsive behaviour does not emerge out of nowhere. The root cause is generally unresolved fear. When fear is not dealt with, it grows, until it is a constant presence that can easily turn into obsessive-compulsive behaviour.

Frankie was referred to my office by a member of Alcoholics Anonymous. Although she had a problem with alcohol, her major issue was washing her hands many, many times a day.

Frankie confided that she had suffered from this obsessive-compulsive illness for almost 20 years. It had grown progressively worse, to the point where her husband was ready to walk out and take their four-year-old son with him.

Because of her compulsion, Frankie's housework consumed her from six or seven in the morning until late at night, and still she didn't feel that everything was clean. She would begin scrubbing the table—washing the same space over and over again. Part way through she would think, "I'm sure I missed a spot," and she would start washing it all over again.

"Sometimes," Frankie confessed, "I spend hours trying to wipe my kitchen counter clean and then I'll just put my head on the counter and cry."

And indeed, the first time Frankie came to my office, that's exactly what she did. She sat in the middle of the floor and cried. "I'm just too tired to do it any more," she sobbed. "And I can't make even the smallest decision. I get others to make them for me. I pester them so much with my problems that none of my friends or relatives want to have anything more to do with me."

Frankie shared that her greatest fear was not getting her hands clean. "I tell myself I can't remember washing them, and I end up washing my hands for six or seven hours at a time, using maybe six bars of soap in the process."

Psychiatrists had tried many different treatments on Frankie, including hospitalization, , LSD, shock treatment, a hypoglycemic diet, vitamin therapy, a variety of tranquilizers, anti-depressants, sleeping pills and other drugs. Nothing helped.

I realized that Frankie needed a miracle that only God could perform. I first helped her see that her hand-washing compulsion was caused by fear and guilt. As we talked more, Frankie admitted she came from a dysfunctional home where her parents had never encouraged her or built up her self-esteem. Hoping to improve herself, she became a nurse. A patient died on her unit, and even though she had done nothing to contribute to the death, Frankie was consumed by the fear that she would eventually make a fatal mistake. In an effort to make sure she would not transfer any disease germs, Frankie became a compulsive hand-washer.

Frankie and I prayed about a number of things, including her relationship with her parents. I gave her scripture that addressed Frankie's specific fears. One verse from God's Word was John 15:3 which says, "You are already clean because of the word which I have spoken to you."

Hebrews 4:12 was also helpful to Frankie, which says that "... the Word of God is living and powerful, and sharper than any two-edged sword, piercing even to the division of soul and spirit, and of joints and marrow, and is a discerner of the thoughts and intents of the heart." I helped Frankie see how this scripture deals with every area in our lives: "the soul" which is the real you; "the spirit" which refers to the relationship we have with God in Christ; "the joints and marrow," the physical part of our selves; "the discerner of the thoughts," speaks of our mental health; and "the intents of the heart" which addresses our emotions and attitudes.

I felt it would be advantageous for Frankie's husband to be involved in her treatment and recovery process, but he was so full of hate because

of all the embarrassment she had caused him that he refused to participate. He was an alcoholic who didn't believe he had a problem. That left
Frankie to deal with her problem on her own.

Frankie began to recognize that faithfulness to Jesus Christ can bring
miracles that transform a person's life. As she meditated on God's Word
and trusted Christ, Frankie was able to start making decisions on her
own. Cleaning her house took less and less time. Instead of standing
at the sink whenever she felt the compulsion to wash her hands, she
would pray. And every time she did, she received the help she needed.

Frankie hadn't known this kind of freedom for twenty years. Major
decisions, like buying rugs and drapes remained difficult, but God gave
her the ability to make these decisions. Eventually, her husband came to
recognize the progress she was making and grew proud of Frankie and
her accomplishments. So did her relatives.

Frankie went on to become a ward clerk in a hospital. Where a few
years before, she was unable to even clean her own house, she was now
able to carry on a good job. It was a tremendous victory.

Anorexia Nervosa and Bulimia

A gentleman approached me after a presentation and asked, "Do you
remember me? You saved my daughter Becky's life." I did remember
him. And I remembered Becky.

Becky was anorexic. Her parents had done everything they knew to
help her, but nothing worked. Their last resort was to bring Becky for
counseling. Anorexia nervosa and bulimia are other common forms of
obsessive-compulsive behaviours. Anorexia nervosa is an illness characterized by an obsession with losing weight. It often leads to peculiar
patterns of handling food, and an intense fear of weight-gain.

I began by telling Becky that her primary problem was fear. Becky
was surprised. "No one as ever told me that before," she said.

Becky feared growing fat, and she feared failure. I knew from talking
with her parents that she was a high school student who would study
for exams until four in the morning, even though she maintained a
98% average.

The first step in guiding Becky to recovery was helping her deal with the extinction of her fear. Today, Becky is school teacher and is happily married with four wonderful children.

So what is the root cause of eating disorders like anorexia and bulimia? Some believe the fault lies with our culture's emphasis on slimness as a condition for attractiveness and social acceptance. Young girls feel pressured to lose weight if they want to be popular in school. They work so hard at being runway model-thin that they develop anorexia. Even after they've starved off 30% of their body weight, they still consider themselves overweight.

Many physicians consider the onset of puberty to be the main trigger for developing anorexia because puberty brings with it a whole new set of social responsibilities. The development of breasts and other body changes can cause a teenage girl to panic and resort to dieting and starvation to try to halt or control the forward movement of her development. Girls who are emotionally unequipped to take steps toward independence will sometimes become excessively childlike and dependent on their parents.

Fears about sexual development and the potential of becoming pregnant are also present in many anorectics. Some wish to avoid sexuality by maintaining a flat, boyish figure.

Studies show that people with eating disorders generally come from families with weight issues. These issues include obesity, a preoccupation with dieting and slimness, and an emphasis on physical beauty as a sign of perfection.

Anorexia nervosa is the third most common chronic illness among adolescents. The typical patient is a teenage girl, although anorectic symptoms may appear from pre-adolescence to the early twenties and thirties. The peak age is between 10 and 15.

Bulimics, on the other hand, crave food and indulge in wild eating binges. They eat incredibly huge amounts—everything from junk food to elaborate meals—and immediately afterward, disgusted by their lack of control, force themselves to vomit. Because they are constantly hungry, they may repeat this procedure several times a day. Once the pattern is set, it is very hard to stop. Some bulimics will resort to laxatives, diuretics and enemas to rid their bodies of the gorged food.

Often, the bulimic overeats to ease guilt, depression, anxiety, or some other emotional problem. Eating (biting, chewing, swallowing) seems to have an emotionally soothing effect, and is a relief from the negative feelings that overwhelm the person. Tension, frustration, loneliness, emptiness and boredom can also lead to eating binges. The abnormal eating habit can become so strong that people have been known to steal to support it.

Spiritual healing for the Anorectic/Bulimic
Starvation is an extreme, incorrect, and unBiblical way to deal with life's problems. If not halted, it is also suicidal.

The food-related symptoms of eating disorders are a sign of other disturbances in mental and social functioning. Common to all is fear of being overweight, when in fact, girls like Becky can become emaciated. This perception persists despite all reason. Eating and physical indulgences are viewed as personal weaknesses. To resist food is to demonstrate absolute control.

Gather sufficient data and find Biblical solutions. Some of the problem areas I have looked for when trying to help young women heal from anorexia and bulimia are:
- **Lack of salvation.** Do they know how much God loves them? Do they know that Jesus came to save them and desires a living relationship with them?
- **UnBiblical husband–wife relationship in parents and in the parent–child relationship.** Mom and dad are not agreed on the spiritual direction of the home. There are no clearly defined roles in the marriage, which causes anxiety and uncertainty for the children. Often one of the parents is harsh and legalistic, and the other one is lax and aloof.
- **UnBiblical view of self, of sex, of authority.** Many who struggle in this area believe God is cruel, judgemental, yet absent and sex is dirty and should be avoided at all cost. This idea comes about because of extreme self-loathing towards their own body. Authority is not to be trusted, because their main intent is to regiment the eating behaviour of the struggling youth or young adult.

- **Manipulation and blame-shifting; not accepting certain aspects of adult responsibility.** Nearly all those that I have counseled who struggle with an obsessive-compulsive behaviour lie to me and others, especially family members who are the most affected by their behaviour. This may seem unfair, but I expect them to try to manipulate me and lie, because that is the pattern in the home. To blame someone else for their problems becomes very instinctual for them. It is easier for them to lie, than to admit that they have a problem.

- **Failure to deal Biblically with anger, worry, fear, or guilt; holding a grudge against someone who has committed an offence; refusing to forgive others.** Resenting others for harsh words, unkind actions gives rise to bitterness. It is my role as a people-helper to encourage forgiving others, even if they believe that person does not deserve to be forgiven. As long as they refuse to forgive, the eating disorder behaviour will continue,

- **Boredom with life.** With many who are controlled by an eating disorder, life has lost its meaning. Bored with life, frustrated with the state they are in, these individuals find solace in the thing that is destroying their lives and relationships.

- **Recent death, illness, separation in the family, or a family move can bring on the eating disorder and certainly escalate the problem if it has been ongoing.** We look for ways to cope when we have experienced a loss in our lives.

When working with an anorectic or bulimic, considerable counseling needs to be done with the parents to deal with any factors that may have contributed to the problem. In many instances, parents have allowed abundant privileges and hold the opinion that anything the child has achieved is "because we gave her everything." Sadly, there is often no genuine interest in the parent-child relationship; the parents don't accept the child as being an individual of worth.

Self-starvation and binge/purge behaviours are directly related to an intense desire for approval and unrealistic achievement expectations. Beneath all of that are issues of poor self-esteem, feelings of helplessness, and the desperate struggle to win power, approval, admiration and respect.

The person must be offered God's hope and help for the problems she is avoiding. The Biblical teaching is that an irresistible urge to eat is a habit, not a physical problem. It is learned behaviour that can be unlearned. The Bible tells us the only addiction we should have is to the Holy Spirit who can replace any power and control sin has over us.

Rose was referred to my office by a doctor who diagnosed her as having anorexia nervosa. Though now 20, Rose's problem began in grade ten when she grew overly sensitive about potential obesity, even though she only weighed 90 pounds. Rose developed the classic anorectic's fear of eating. She was lonely and depressed and had few friends. Rose would eat in the evenings, and then feel very guilty about it.

Rose's father disclosed that when his daughter was in grade twelve, she was abnormally fearful of failing and had studied seven days a week. Even though she graduated with a 96% average, like Becky, Rose was still not satisfied with her academic performance.

Rose was a Christian, but she was frustrated by her lack of progress in dealing with this illness. She interpreted it as proof that God was unable to help her. In fact, Rose was convinced that the intense fear she was experiencing was God's way of punishing her. I assured her that just the opposite was true, God wanted to alleviate the difficulties that controlled her.

It was evident to me that Rose suffered from guilt, fear, depression, and a very poor self image. Since she believed her fear came from God, it was necessary to show her from the Bible that Satan, not God, was the source of her fear.

We examined 2 Timothy 1:7 which says, "God has not given us a spirit of fear; but of power and of love, and of a sound mind." I explained that according to some commentators and Biblical scholars, the original Greek explains the phrase "spirit of fear" as "evil spirit of fear." I assured her that God gives the opposite of fear: power, love and a sound mind. Rose had an immediate and positive response to that Biblical principle. Rose also needed to realize that God loved her and was not out to destroy her.

The words of Jesus Christ became very specific to her situation. Jesus gives a call, a prerequisite, and a promise when He says in Matthew 11:28-30, "Come unto me, all ye that labour and are heavy laden, and I will give you rest. Take My yoke upon you and learn from Me; for I am gentle and lowly of heart: and you will find rest for your souls. For My yoke is easy, and My burden is light." Jesus is the one who does the calling. When we are burdened down with fear, guilt, resentment or loss, we seem to be immobilized to reach out to God, so He reaches out to us. The prerequisite or necessity is: we have to come to Him, we must let Him carry our burdens and we must desire to learn of Jesus and His love. Jesus promises that He will give us His rest and He will lighten our heavy load. I have found it so amazing that as individuals come to Christ in repentance and humility, immediately things begin to change in their lives.

Rose agreed that she needed a rest from her constant labouring and the heaviness of heart and spirit she was experiencing.

In subsequent sessions, we examined Rose's damaged self-esteem in the light of God's Word. Chapter eight of Paul's letter to the Romans has much to say about God's love and the fact that there is no condemnation from God's viewpoint. "There is therefore now no condemnation to them which are in Christ Jesus, who walk not after the flesh, but after the Spirit. For the law of the Spirit of life in Christ Jesus has made me free from the law of sin and death" (Romans 8: 1, 2).

Once Rose realized that God was really on her side and not against her, she opened up in other areas, as well.

I offered Rose specific Bible verses to memorize and bring to mind whenever she was tempted to cave in to fear, guilt, depression, or feelings of low self-worth. I also challenged her to become involved with other Christian believers her age and to push forward in the areas that had previously defeated her.

> **Here are some of the Bible verses that can help people like Rose recover from anorectic compulsions:**
>
> "Or do you not know that your body is the temple of the Holy Spirit who is in you, whom you have from God, and you are not your own? For you were bought at a price; therefore glorify God in your body and in your spirit, which are God's" (1 Corinthians 6: 19, 20).
>
> "Therefore, whether you eat or drink, or whatever you do, do all to the glory of God" (1 Corinthians 10: 31).
>
> "Nothing is better for a man than that he should eat and drink, and that his soul should enjoy good in his labor. This also, I saw, was from the hand of God. For who can eat, or who can have enjoyment, more than I?" (Ecclesiastes 2: 24, 25).
>
> "... every man should eat and drink and enjoy the good of all his labor—it is a gift of God" (Ecclesiastes 3: 13).
>
> "Do not let your adornment be merely outward—arranging the hair, wearing gold, or putting on fine apparel—rather let it be the hidden person of the heart, with the incorruptible beauty of a gentle and quiet spirit, which is very precious in the sight of God" (1 Peter 3: 3,4).

Rose was faithful in allowing Jesus to become Lord of her life and in accepting the Bible as God's truth for her. She conscientiously did the Bible homework I assigned. By the time our several months of counseling had ended, Rose had gained twenty pounds and was a vibrant witness for Jesus Christ. Once Rose found healing from her fear and compulsive anorectic behaviour, she had no desire to return to the bondage that had formerly controlled her.

Rose was soon invited to share her testimony with a women's group with more than two hundred members. During her talk, Rose gave glory to Jesus Christ for the victory she had achieved. This was truly a miracle. Eight months earlier, Rose would have been much too fearful to relate even to a small group.

Alcoholism

Alcoholism is another type of obsessive-compulsive behaviour. Society's most common legal drug, alcohol is a malevolent killer physically, emotionally, mentally, and spiritually. An anonymous writer produced this credo for alcohol: "I am more powerful than the combined armies of the world; I have destroyed more men than all the wars of the nations; I have caused millions of accidents and wrecked more homes than all the floods, tornadoes, and hurricanes put together. I find victims among the rich and poor alike, the young and old, the strong and weak; I loom in such proportions that I cast a shadow over every field of labour; I am relentless, insidious, unpredictable; I am everywhere—in the home, on the street, in the factory, in the office, on the sea, and in the air; I bring sickness, poverty and death. I give nothing and take all; I am your worst enemy; I am ALCOHOL!"

I know about alcoholism firsthand because it destroyed my own family. My father was a heavy drinker who eventually became an alcoholic. Instead of his wages going to feed and clothe his family, it was squandered on booze. My mother also became an alcoholic. While we children were still living with her, she lived with men who were angry and bitter and drank heavily. Having us taken away almost certainly drove her deeper into that lifestyle. Her fatal accident was alcohol related.

What is alcoholism?

A vast majority of alcohol drinkers are able to control their intake. They can drink to the point where they feel they've had enough and then stop. A small percentage of individuals however, become dependent on alcohol and are unable to deny the urge to drink. There are also those who use alcohol to find relief from feelings of anxiety, inadequacy, loneliness, depression, and the like. Others look to alcohol for escape from unbearable pressures, stress, and personal problems. Some just have a compulsion to drink.

Alcoholism is a condition in which the individual drinks compulsively to the point of intoxication over and over again. The compulsive drinker keeps on drinking regardless of the cost to health, job, and family.

Alcoholism is a slowly progressive illness that may take five to twenty years before its victim becomes unemployable or is incapable of being a responsible employee or family member. If untreated, alcoholism ends (with few exceptions) in permanent mental damage, physical incapacity, or early death.

Who are alcoholics?

Most people's stereotypical alcoholic is a skid-row derelict, but alcoholism is not restricted to any one segment of society. The disease is no respecter of persons. Most people with alcoholism have families, hold regular jobs, and may not appear to be much different from anyone else. Some even stand behind pulpits Sunday after Sunday.

What causes alcoholism?

The cause of alcoholism has yet to be conclusively determined, but the prevailing view is two-fold. The physical view is that some people are born with a specific physical vulnerability to the physiological effects of alcohol. Because of this vulnerability, their reaction to alcohol is more intense than that of others and they develop a greater need for alcohol—a need that becomes an obsession and ultimately an addiction. The propensity for the disease may be present, but lies dormant until the susceptible individual begins to drink. Then the pre-determined, predictable process is triggered.

People who become alcoholics can also be alcoholism-prone because of psychological factors. These are people who in childhood went through deeply disturbing emotional experiences such as rejection by parents, parental cruelty and abuse, inability to make friends, lack of success in school, lack of fulfilment and gratification, constant parental conflict, alcoholism in the family, or a broken home, to name a few. As a result of these distressing influences, such individuals developed feelings of anxiety, insecurity, depression, loneliness, intense anger, low self-esteem, which they carry into adolescence and adult life. They may also have personality traits that limit their capacity to deal realistically with emotional pain. They discover that alcohol can produce euphoria, inflate the deflated ego, beautify the ugly self-image, and distort reality so the drinker does not have to deal with it.

In all my professional experience, I have never worked with an alcoholic who was not fearful and guilt-ridden. Every one of them had a dismally low self-worth and was resentful and angry.

Research has shown certain personality traits that are common to alcoholics, including dependence, fearfulness, anxiety and resentment. The alcoholic has difficulty making decisions, is self-centered and filled with self-pity. Anger, dishonesty, and lack of tolerance may also be present, as well as a tendency to demand perfection from everyone but himself.

Many of these traits were evident in the chaos of Jim and Diane's home. The couple had been married for about twelve years before our counseling sessions began. Jim and Diane had marriage problems. Alcoholism was a major factor in the home, but it was difficult to assess whether the alcohol created the other problems or the crushing problems contributed to the alcoholism.

Jim was extremely fearful, and had a serious inferiority complex. He felt uncontrolled hatred for others, including his wife. He attributed his fear, insecurity, and resentment to being belittled as a child by his father.

Diane, on the other hand, was disorganized to the point of mental confusion. She was also a screamer, hypersensitive, and extremely selfish and unloving.

Jim and Diane had both made commitments to Jesus Christ, but experienced little victory in their spiritual lives. It was obvious there was no simple fix for their situation. A variety of counseling techniques would have to be used to deal with their problems.

The Fifth Step is one of the key sessions in the Alcoholics Anonymous program. During this step, the one being counseled articulates everything that is troubling him, thus providing the counselor with pertinent information necessary to determine what needs to be done to alleviate the client's stress. Jim was very open. He admitted he had deep-seated problems with fear and an inability to cope with everyday life. He also had resentment toward his wife, his parents and his in-laws. Jim harboured guilt over pre-marital sexual relationships, masturbation, and erotic sex acts that he felt were outside of God's plan for married couples.

Since fear of people was Jim's biggest problem, we created a strategy to deal with these fears. I encouraged Jim's involvement with other individuals and small groups of people. Part of the plan was Jim's taking full responsibility for a youth hockey team, mingling with people in a shopping mall, spending time in coffee shops regardless of the number of people present, participating in a small Bible study group and attending church on Sundays where he was required to meet and interact with other people.

Several strategies were used with Diane who was hypersensitive, moody and depressed. These included referral to a local medical doctor (who discovered Diane had severe hypoglycemia) and participation in family counseling sessions. During her Fifth Step processing, Diane revealed her own resentments, as well as her guilt over pre-marital sex relationships, masturbation, screaming at her children, stealing, and showing very little love. After several sessions, she seemed to be able to talk about and work on correcting the sexual situations and was prepared to work at restitution for her stealing.

Our family counseling sessions dealt with the spiritual domain. Jim and Diane aired their issues and I helped them begin working on the issues. The Love Chapter, 1 Corinthians 13, became a foundational scripture passage for them both.

Jim and Diane were also encouraged to spend more time together, to talk over issues that were causing strife in their home, and to participate in ongoing individual or joint counseling sessions.

Jim, who knew he would have to be accountable to his counselor after each part of the fear-extinction plan, completed each stage successfully. He was very satisfied with his efforts to gain victory over his fear of people. Diane, on the other hand, was half-hearted about sticking to her diet and treatment, and about her commitment to the Biblical principles that would have alleviated much of the stress in the home. Though they had been given the tools to live each day victoriously, they only saw success as long as they put Christ first. When they refused to recognize the lordship of Jesus Christ, past problems once again surfaced and their marriage never became healthy even until this day.

The case of Tim and Marilyn

When I met Tim and Marilyn, they were on the verge of separation because of alcoholism. Tim had been promiscuous during his drinking days and indulged in sexual fantasies and masturbation. Now guilt was making him impotent during the sex act, something that made Marilyn so angry and frustrated she wanted to end the marriage. But Marilyn had issues of her own. She was extremely introverted, resentful, had a poor self-image, and was troubled by extended periods of depression.

Tim's lack of love for himself, his wife and his children (plus his overly aggressive devotion to his business) had seriously damaged their marriage and his relationship with his family. Both he and Marilyn realized their children were being hurt by their extremely strained relationship. They wanted to change.

The actual therapy for Tim and Marilyn began at a young couples' retreat. During the retreat, Tim and Marilyn committed their lives to Jesus Christ. Unfortunately, that did not mean that all the problems of their past were immediately gone. But a new spiritual beginning is always the very best way to start mending a broken relationship.

Since medical experts who study alcoholism believe there is a strong correlation between alcoholism and hypoglycemia, one of the very first steps prescribed for both Tim and Marilyn was a visit to a physician. Research suggests there are similarities in the biochemical makeup of individuals affected by both disorders. Even when an alcoholic stops drinking, he may still be plagued by issues with hypoglycemia. Unchecked, hypoglycemia gives rise to thought, mood, and perception distortion. As it turned out, both Tim and Marilyn were severe hypoglycemics. Their physician prescribed a high protein, low carbohydrate diet along with specific vitamin supplements.

I encouraged Tim and Marilyn to be faithful in attending church and Bible studies. The Bible studies moved them from a brand new walk with Christ to being aware and responsive to the work of the Holy Spirit in their individual lives. This enabled them to witness to others about how they'd found salvation through Jesus Christ.

Since Tim's sexual problems were very deep-rooted, I assigned him specific Biblical lessons to be done on a consistent basis. He was required to memorize 2 Corinthians 10:3-5 and apply the principles.

These verses encourage the reader to cast down evil imaginings and turn all evil thoughts over to Jesus Christ. Tim needed this mental exercise for spiritual victory over his sexual fantasies.

I also asked Tim to read chapters six, seven and eight of Romans, to record each time the Bible used the phrase "free from sin" or "free from bondage," and to express verbally why he was now free from sin. The purpose of this homework was to reinforce that victory was his in Jesus Christ.

Marilyn had a lot of difficulty getting over her resentment regarding Tim's rejection and lack of love, but as she and Tim became faithfully involved in the Bible study, prayer group, and church worship, they were both able to overcome their drinking problems and rebuild their marriage and home life.

Consider these helpful Biblical teachings that apply to the alcoholic.

Luke 21: 34–36: Jesus warns Christians to be on guard against being caught in their old habits.

Galatians 5:21–24: Be filled with God's personality, the fruit of the Holy Spirit.

Ephesians 5:18: Getting drunk with wine is a foolish pleasure. Instead, be filled with the Holy Spirit.

Romans 13:13–14: Be continually involved with Jesus and His Word.

Proverbs 28:13: The alcoholic must confess and forsake his way.

Romans 14:21: Realize there are others who are looking at us for Christian guidance.

1 John 2:15–17: Do the will of God and you will be delivered from the desire to follow your lust.

Revelation 1:4–8: We are released from our bondage by the blood of Jesus, so get excited about that and look for Jesus' coming. It will be soon.

As a counselor, I have found The Twelve Steps of Alcoholics Anonymous to be extremely useful in dealing with those who seek to overcome the alcoholic personality.

THE TWELVE STEPS OF ALCOHOLICS ANONYMOUS

1. We admitted we were powerless over alcohol—that our lives had become unmanageable.

2. Came to believe that a Power greater than ourselves could restore us to sanity.

3. Made a decision to turn our will and our lives over to the care of God as we understood Him.

4. Made a searching and fearless moral inventory of ourselves.

5. Admitted to God, to ourselves, and to another human being the exact nature of our wrongs.

6. Were entirely ready to have God remove all these defects of character.

7. Humbly asked Him to remove our shortcomings.

8. Made a list of all persons we had harmed, and became willing to make amends to them all.

9. Made direct amends to such people wherever possible, except when to do so would injure them or others.

10. Continued to take personal inventory and when we were wrong promptly admitted it.

11. Sought through prayer and meditation to improve our conscious contact with God, as we understood Him, praying only

for knowledge of His will for us and the power to carry that out.

12. Having had a spiritual awakening as the result of these Steps, we tried to carry this message to alcoholics, and to practice these principles in all our affairs.

As these Twelve Steps teach, the alcoholic needs to recognize his need for God in a personal way. The alcoholic is taught that alcoholism stems from wrong thinking, such as fear, guilt, and resentment. The person's thinking must be changed from negativism to a thought life that is rooted in the truth of Scripture. Specific procedures need to be followed to renew his mind. These might include thinking about and meditating on God's Word, particularly these passages: "You will keep him in perfect peace whose mind is stayed on You, because he trusts in You" (Isaiah 26:3). "Then Jesus said, 'If you abide in My word, you are My disciples indeed. And you shall know the truth, and the truth shall make you free'...I say to you, whoever commits sin is a slave of sin. And a slave does not abide in the house forever, but a son abides forever. Therefore, if the Son makes you free, you shall be free indeed" (John 8: 31, 32; 34–36). "The thief does not come except to steal, and to kill, and to destroy. I have come that they may have life and that they may have it more abundantly" (John 10:10).

> **If you or someone you love struggles with alcohol abuse, spend time considering these passages as well.**
>
> Psalms 1:1-3; 16:11; 51:10; 100:1-5; 103:1-5
> Romans 8:1-2, 31-39; 6:10-20
> 2 Corinthians 10:3-5
> Ephesians: 4:17-32; 6:10-20
> Colossians 3:1-17
> Philippians 2:5-11; 4:4-8, 13, 19
> 2 Timothy 1:7
> 1 John 5:4-5

To be controlled by any obsession is one of the worst traumas for any individual to cope with, whether it is the compulsive behaviour of alcoholism, rechecking everything, hand-washing, collecting and hoarding, or anorectic or bulimic behaviours. Satan wreaks havoc on the person with obsessive-compulsive tendencies or the individual with a predisposition to act or react in a certain way. That's because Satan's whole mission is to destroy every person he possibly can. Jesus warned us of this in his statement: "The thief does not come except to steal, and to kill and to destroy..." (John 10:10). Jesus Christ, on the other hand, sets people free through His power and the power of the Word of God.

Prayer:
"I have been eaten up, devoured, obsessed and consumed with anxieties and fears. I keep doing things I don't want to do: again, and again, and again. I confess, Lord, I can't stop on my own. You know I've tried. Your Word tells me that the Holy Spirit gives me fruit—or evidence—of Your character within me: 'love, joy, peace, patience, kindness, goodness, faithfulness, gentleness and self control,' especially self-control (Galatians 5:22). Spirit of the Almighty, living, breathing, restoring God, have mercy on my sin and liberate me from the grip of obsessions and compulsions so I can live in the freedom of self-control. I release to You the benefits of my fixations, 'for it is for freedom that Christ has set me free. Therefore, I will not be burdened again by a yoke of slavery...for the mind controlled by the Spirit is life and peace!' (Galatians 5:1 and Romans 8:6b). Amen."

CHAPTER 8: CAVING IN: DEPRESSION

Maria's children are grown and have moved on to careers, spouses, and travelling the world. Maria talks to them on the telephone and follows their exploits on Facebook, but she feels painfully separated from them. Her husband left when the children were small and Maria poured herself into creating and maintaining a loving home for them. Now she feels abandoned and alone.

Angry, negative thoughts constantly swirl in her mind. She is still furious at her husband, and now feels betrayed by her children for living their lives without her. Friends avoid Maria because all she talks about is how dismal her life is. Her boss has confronted her about her attitude at work, something that only increases Maria's bitter thoughts. She continues going to work only because she needs the money.

Maria has withdrawn from community activities. Her weight has increased dramatically and she feels tired all the time. She can't keep dark thoughts and helpless feelings from overwhelming her. She can't see any way out. Maria is depressed.

Josh is a young man who appears to have everything a person could want. He completed university, has a good job, a new car, and is well-liked. What people don't know is that Josh struggles with periods of deep depression. He will sleep for what seems like days at a time, eating very little and feeling as if he's been sucked into a black hole. He will call in sick for work, but no one knows the real reason.

To keep the depression at bay, Josh is taking illicit substances, but they only make the low periods worse. He hasn't told anyone what's really happening in his life, and that increases his feelings of loneliness and isolation.

Josh believes he is the only one suffering in a world of success, influence, and frenzied happiness.

When Cathy was nine, she became withdrawn, despondent and depressed over the death of her sister eighteen months earlier. She admits to spending a lot of time writing letters to her sister in heaven and going through her sister's cards and clothing. Those activities only make her feel more depressed. In an attempt to bring Cathy some relief from her loneliness, her parents adopted a girl her age. Cathy grew hostile and aggressive toward the new family member.

Rachel is a 28-year-old client who came from a religious home. Alcoholism, incest, and beatings were a regular part of her experience growing up. As an adult, she began using drugs and alcohol to numb the pain of her past. Rachel is deeply depressed because her children have been removed from the home due to her drug and alcohol abuse. Rachel is a new Christian, but is still depressed over her inability to get her children back.

Yvonne has always been considered a strong woman. She was influential in the lives of her children who have all left home—a home where there has always been a certain amount of legalism and tradition interwoven with a Christian veneer. At 50, Yvonne is suffering from menopausal depression that has lasted for months. Her suicidal thoughts make her fear she's losing her salvation, and because of her inability to get over the depression, she has a dismal opinion of herself.

These stories are all examples of how depression might look for different people. My own personal time of depression came after I attended my girlfriend's graduation. I went with the idea of enjoying her moment of achievement, but when I saw the graduates filing across the platform, accepting the symbol of their achievement, it suddenly hit me! I had blown it. I had dropped out. I would never graduate from high school.

In that moment, I felt I was a total failure, and I became deeply depressed. When you've come from nothing and have nothing, lacking an education makes you feel as if you are even more of a loser.

My way of handling my depression initially was to go out and get drunk. Then I poured myself into my job to deaden my feelings. My job was working at a chicken ranch where I spent my days cleaning pens, slaughtering and eviscerating the old poultry—not very glamorous work. My salvation came quite literally and completely the following year when I gave my life to the Lord and returned to school.

What Is Depression?

The term depression is tossed around rather frivolously in our society. How often do you hear someone use it in reference to a mild disappointment or some trivial dissatisfaction, like "I've put on ten pounds...I'm so depressed"? This is not true depression. Genuine depression affects every part of a person's life and being.

Some of the latest statistics indicate that one in six North American adults has been diagnosed with depression, or will become depressed at some point. Because these statistics took into consideration only those who sought medical attention for depression, I believe the number is probably much, much higher.

A recent Ipsos Reid poll on depression in the workplace found that 18% of Canadians and 20% of Americans say they have been diagnosed with depression. Overall, 26% of respondents in Canada, and more than that in the U.S., say they are either clinically depressed or think they are, but have never been properly diagnosed. Interestingly, more women than men are affected and depression is more prevalent among those with lower income and less education.

Depression drains the North American economy of nearly $300 billion annually through lost productivity and the added burden on the medical system.

Three Kinds of Depression

There are three kinds of depression. Each one affects us in four areas (mentally, physically, emotionally, and spiritually), and is accompanied by noticeable symptoms.

Mild depression, or discouragement, may be characterized by self-doubt, self-pity or resentment, loss of appetite, sleeplessness, and an unkempt appearance. Emotionally, the person feels sad, discontent, and irritable. From a spiritual standpoint, they may question or be displeased with God's will.

In **moderate depression,** there is a sense of despondency. Anger, self-criticism and self-pity may combine with apathy, hypochondria, and a tendency toward "the weeps." The person is emotionally distressed, sorrowful, lonely, and angry at God, perhaps griping at God or outright rejecting God's will.

Severe depression is accompanied by despair, bitterness, self-rejection, and self-pity. Physically, there may be withdrawal, passivity, even catatonia. The severely depressed person experiences hopelessness, abandonment, and schizophrenia. Spiritually, there is resentment toward God's Word, indifference, and perhaps unbelief in the Word.

Characteristics of Depression
In his book, *The Secret Strength of Depression*, Fourth Edition (used by permission), Dr. Frederic Flach MD, KCHS, identified ten of the most common characteristics of depression as:
1. General overall feeling of hopelessness, despair, and sadness.
2. Loss of perspective (of job, life, family).
3. Changes in physical acts like eating, sleeping, sex.
4. Loss of self-esteem; self-confidence at an all-time low.
5. Withdrawal from others; a groundless fear of rejection.
6. A desire to escape from problems and life; suicidal thoughts.
7. Overly sensitive to what others say and do, irritable, cries easily.
8. Difficulty handling emotions, especially anger.
9. Guilt is usually present, either real or imagined.
10. Dependence on others, which reinforces a sense of hopelessness.

Depression can best be understood on a continuum that begins with discouragement, escalates to despondency, and culminates in despair. Realizing that depression is an emotion most of us will experience at one time or another, it is important to recognize when we are most vulnerable, and make ourselves aware of possible contributors. Our path to spiritual healing becomes smoother when we understand better the road we are walking upon.

Physical contributors

- mismanagement of health; being physically run down, fatigued or ill; lack of proper diet, exercise and rest; substance abuse (marijuana, alcohol, tobacco); decreased ability to process environmental toxins
- infections of the brain, nervous system, or body
- adverse reactions to or side-effects from medication
- genetic predisposition to any of the following physical conditions: PMS (premenstrual syndrome); glandular disorders; imbalance of secretions from the adrenal or pituitary glands; thyroid problems; diabetes or hypoglycemia; malabsorption of certain essential vitamins (anaemia, vitamin B deficiency, etc).
- inherited tendencies toward depression (parental, social modeling, poor ways of coping with stress)
- developmental factors like menopause

Mental contributors

- destructive thought patterns or habits, generally in response to stress, (Christmas, for example); low self-image; idealism; perfectionism; self-absorption and introspective thinking
- inability to forget painful memories (unresolved anger; unwillingness to forgive)

Emotional contributors

- emotional response to traumatic events (child abuse, incest, rape, etc.)
- emotional reactions to loss (death, health, job, material security, etc.)
- intense feelings of guilt and inadequacy, self-pity and anger

Social contributors

- loss of meaningful relationships: friendships, marital separation, job loss

Spiritual (moral) contributors

- failure to attain a standard of conduct or spiritual goal. (The standard may be established by self, significant others, or by God)
- perfectionism
- hypocritical behaviour
- feelings of condemnation (real or false guilt)
- attacks from Satan

Achieving Success

These causes are fairly easy to understand and relate to, but a less obvious cause of depression is achieving success. Philip was a university professor who was so depressed that when he came home from work every day, all he wanted to do was lie on his bed in the dark. He had no friends, didn't feel good about his job, his marriage, or himself, even though many would envy all that Philip had achieved.

Philip needed to talk out his fears and anxieties, and build himself up with regular scripture reading and prayer. He also needed a friend, so I connected him with a Christian colleague. Gradually he was able to find healing and purpose and meaning in his life.

When I was studying for my Ph.D., someone said, "Bruce, be careful you don't crack when you're finished." When one has striven exceptionally hard and put a lot of effort into completing a major challenge, the achievement can seem disappointingly anti-climactic. Rather than being relieved and revelling in the achievement, the person may feel strangely adrift and depressed.

Guilt

Guilt is another cause of depression. In some cases, the guilt is real, in other cases, it is imagined. It may be guilt over something done, or something left undone. In some cases, people stay sunk in depression because they feel they benefit from the depression. They enjoy receiving people's sympathy and refuse to deal with the depression. When a person begins being depressed, he generally behaves in a way that reinforces the depression. Instead of dealing with the negative state of mind, his actions lead him into a deeper and more dangerous condition, making lasting spiritual healing even more difficult to achieve.

What We Need

Maslow's Hierarchy of Human Needs is a psychology theory proposed by American psychologist Abraham Maslow. It is often portrayed in the shape of a pyramid with the most fundamental levels of need on the bottom. These basic needs are esteem (feeling competent and obtaining social approval), interpersonal connection (acceptance and love), security, and physical needs (food, water). Maslow's theory contends that until these most basic needs are met, the individual will not strongly desire secondary or higher level needs like cognitive needs (to explore, understand and know), a desire for beauty (in art, music, etc.), and self-actualization or functioning at your fullest potential. According to Maslow, if basic esteem and interpersonal needs are not met, depression will result.

Stress and Depression

There is a direct correlation between stress and depression. In their book, *The Stress Factor*, psychiatrists Frank Minirth and Paul Meier state that while a certain amount of stress is common, over a period of time stress can cause burnout and excessive burnout without the application of coping techniques will, without question, lead to clinical depression.

The authors offer the example of two women who were treated for suicidal depression in their psychiatric clinic. Both were consumed with bitterness and unforgiveness which contributed to emotional burnout and eventually to deep depression. The two women had similar backgrounds: both were eldest children; exhibited strong musical talents at an early age and continued to develop and use them in adulthood; and were involved in a teaching career. As well, both had been sexually and emotionally abused at an early age by their fathers and by other male family members.

Both women experienced severe burnout as wives and mothers. In both cases, the consciousness of what had happened to them as young girls surfaced when the counselors compassionately removed the blocks that had led to their severe depression. One, although appropriately angry, chose to forgive her father and the others for what had happened. She was able to recover and experience personal restoration. The other retained a measure of bitterness and resentment. She failed to achieve the same measure of recovery.

Depression does not play favourites. It can hit women, men, children—even senior citizens—in equally devastating frequency.

How To Guard Against Depression

In *None of These Diseases: The Bible's Health Secrets for the 21st Century* (Revell, 2000), S. I. McMillen states a profound truth: "Since we have shown that our attitudes of mind are more important than the daily insults of life, it is important that we condition our minds before life's major catastrophes hit us."

Many psychologists have compiled stress index charts listing the most disturbing events one can encounter in life. Among those that can cause depression are:

1. Death of a child
2. Death of a spouse
3. A jail sentence
4. An unfaithful spouse
5. Major financial difficulty
6. Business failure
7. Being fired
8. Miscarriage/stillbirth
9. Divorce/marital separation
10. Court appearance
11. Unwanted pregnancy
12. Major illness in the family
13. Unemployment for long periods
14. Death of a close friend
15. A demotion
16. Major personal illness

17. Start of an extra-marital affair
18. Loss of personal valuable objects
19. A lawsuit
20. Academic failure
21. Child marries without family approval
22. Broken engagement
23. Taking out a large loan
24. Child going into the armed forces

Unfortunately, when people start to become depressed, they usually behave in a way that reinforces the depression. Instead of dealing with the state of mind they are in, their actions lead them into a deeper condition. The better choice is to be pro-active.

When you feel blue or depressed:

1. Go to bed and sleep as many hours as you can and want to. You may wake up feeling fine.
2. Get some physical exercise, particularly if physical activity has not been a regular part of your life.
3. If you are female, determine if you could be experiencing premenstrual depression. If that is a possibility, take it easy, relax as much as you can, and don't try to force yourself to do unnecessary things which will cause more stress and tension.
4. If the depression persists, have a physical checkup. You may have a medical condition that can be rectified.

Renewing your mind is very important to overcoming depression. In order to renew our mind and have right thinking, we need to remind ourselves of some Biblical injunctions that will be helpful. One key text to consider is Philippians 2:5-11, in which the Apostle Paul says we should have the mind of Christ. The Psalmist David also shares in Psalm 139 how important it is to recognize who we are in God Our Father and in Christ.

Right behaviour is also critical in alleviating depression. Depression may result from guilt over things we have done or are doing that create hardship for us or for others. If that's the case, we need to stop doing the negative things and begin replacing them with positive behaviour. Maybe we need to stop withdrawing and rejecting people and begin cultivating relationships that are meaningful.

Some of the following points I picked up from teaching colleagues at Seminary. We need to strive for good mental health. People with good mental health are not bowled over by their emotions; they take life's disappointments in stride and are able to deal with most situations that come their way. When problems arise, they do something about them. People with good mental health can laugh at themselves. They derive satisfaction from simple everyday pleasures. People with good mental health have self-respect. They don't over-estimate or under-estimate their abilities. People with good mental health are able to give love and consider the interests of others. In doing so, they develop long-lasting, satisfying personal relationships.

Those with good mental health respect the many differences in people. They don't push people around, nor do they allow themselves to be pushed around. They feel part of a group, and have a sense of responsibility toward their neighbours and others. They expect that when they like and trust someone, they will be liked and trusted in return. They accept their responsibilities. Whenever possible, they shape their environment and adjust to it when necessary. People with good mental health plan ahead and do not fear the future. They welcome new ideas and experiences. They set realistic goals for themselves and are able to think for themselves and make their own decisions. They put their best effort into what they do and get satisfaction from doing it. When there is poor mental health, depression is almost inevitable.

How to deal with depression

By the time we reach adulthood, most of us have experienced some sort of hurt in our life. We may not have experienced the death of a child or a spouse, but we have grieved a loss of some kind, and the loss made us feel deeply depressed.

Sometimes depression is linked to bad things that have happened to us. We may lose a friend, or a job; we may have been physically, emotionally, or spiritually hurt. We may feel we are in an impossible financial or relational situation; we may feel isolated and uncared for by those we believe should care for us. We feel that no one understands.

Perhaps we talked about it to a spouse, a friend, a parent, or a pastor who seemed not to care. It usually isn't that people do not care, but rather, they feel helpless to support you in your depression. They simply don't know what to say or do, and in an effort to be helpful, people will often say things that only make us feel worse. They say things like: "You just need to get over this," or "Stop being so self-centered—other people are going through worse," or "Pray more," "Exercise more," "Get out more." We might even try their advice, but it doesn't help. In fact, it makes us feel even more hopeless.

The good news is that we can take our difficult situations and our helplessness and hopelessness to God. He understands because He is an emotional being. We know that because we are emotional beings and the Bible tells us that we are made in God's image: "God said, "Let Us make man in Our image, according to Our likeness..." (Genesis 1:26).

Not only does God understand how we feel, He responds to our suffering and He helps. God cares more than we can imagine. He cares that you are hurting and depressed. God isn't surprised by depression. It's a recurring theme in the Bible. There are a multitude of references in His Word about depression and providing hope.

One such passage is Hebrews 4:13-16: "And there is no creature hidden from His sight, but all things are naked and open to the eyes of Him to whom we must give account. Seeing then that we have a great High Priest who has passed through the heavens, Jesus the Son of God, let us hold fast our confession. For we do not have a High Priest who cannot sympathize with our weaknesses, but was in all points tempted as we are, yet was without sin. Let us therefore come boldly to the throne of grace, that we may obtain mercy and find grace to help in time of need."

Jesus' words in Matthew 11:28-30 are an invitation to us in our pain: "Come to me, all you who are weary and burdened, and I will give you rest. Take my yoke upon you and learn from me, for I am gentle and humble in heart, and you will find rest for your souls. For my yoke is easy and my burden is light" (NIV).

There is also comfort and healing in the well-loved Psalm 23, "The Lord is my shepherd; I shall not want. He maketh me to lie down in green pastures. He leadeth me beside the still water. He restoreth my soul: He leadeth me in the paths of righteousness for His name's sake. Yea, though I walk through the valley of the shadow of death, I will fear no evil: for Thou art with me. Thy rod and Thy staff they comfort me. Thou preparest a table before me in the presence of mine enemies: Thou anointest my head with oil; my cup runneth over. Surely goodness and mercy shall follow me all the days of my life: and I will dwell in the house of the Lord forever" (KJV).

Depression is *not* a sin

Some Christians believe that depression is a sin. It is not. The causes of depression may be sin, but the depression itself is not a sin. Christians do get depressed.

There are numerous examples in the Bible of people who grew depressed because of the sin in their lives. One was King David of Israel. His sin began when he took his eyes off God and committed adultery with another man's wife, and then murdered her husband to try and cover up his own sin.

David's heart-felt lament in Psalm 38 shows an exceedingly lonely, broken, depressed man almost on the verge of death. Ken Taylor's *The Living Bible* presents David's dilemma of self-loathing and fear of death in these words: "O Lord, don't punish me while You are angry. Your arrows have struck deep; Your blows are crushing me. Because of Your anger my body is sick, my health is broken beneath my sins. They are like a flood, higher than my head; they are a burden too heavy to bear. My wounds are festering and full of pus. Because of my sins, I am bent and racked with pain. My days are filled with anguish. My loins burn with inflammation and my whole body is diseased. I am exhausted and crushed; I groan in despair. Lord, you know how I long for my health once more. You hear my every sigh. My heart beats wildly, my strength fails, and I am going blind. My loved ones and friends stay away fearing my disease. Even my own family stands at a distance."

Elijah is another Old Testament figure who experienced deep depression. After the miraculous demonstration of God's power on

Mount Carmel, his footrace with King Ahab's chariot to Jezreel, and Queen Jezebel's threat to murder Elijah, this man of God ran for his life (1 Kings 19:4 says he ran a day's journey into the wilderness). Can you imagine how physically exhausted Elijah must have been? He was certainly depressed. He sat down under a broom tree and prayed that he might die. "It is enough!" Elijah said to God. "Now, Lord, take my life, for I am no better than my fathers!" After some rest, food, and water, the depression passed and he was ready for his next adventure with the Lord.

Depression just may be a God-given defence mechanism to protect us from harm. Depression is a scream, a sigh, or a message that there is something wrong biochemically, physically, emotionally, spiritually, or mentally that needs attention. Once we see depression as a message, we need to respond to that message as soon as possible.

Overcoming depression

The first step, if you are experiencing extreme distress or any suicidal symptoms is to contact a medical professional. Research and experience has shown that good medical treatment, along with appropriate counseling, is the best treatment approach for depression. When it comes to choosing a counselor, find one who is a dedicated Christian. If possible, choose one who has had graduate level training and supervision and preferably one who is certified or licensed by a regulatory body. Many people claim to be counselors; not all are good ones.

You can contribute to your healing and recovery by identifying the wrong thoughts and feelings that leave you vulnerable. God does not want us to be controlled or overwhelmed by wrong or negative emotions like fear, guilt, poor self-image, resentment, bitterness, or depression. Instead, He wants us to experience His love, to have His peace and joy. The Bible underscores this in Romans 12:1, 2, "Therefore, I urge you, brothers, in view of God's mercy, to offer your bodies as a living sacrifice, holy and pleasing to God—which is your spiritual worship. Do not conform any longer to the pattern of this world, but be transformed by the renewing of your mind. Then you will be able to test and approve what God's will is—His good, pleasing and perfect will" (NIV).

The Apostle Paul gave good direction when he wrote: "Finally, brothers, whatever is true, whatever is noble, whatever is right, whatever is pure, whatever is lovely, whatever is admirable—if anything is excellent or praiseworthy—think about such things" (Philippians 4:8, 9, NIV).

Make a positive choice

You can choose to stop dwelling on those thoughts that cause you to feel defeated and unable to look forward to the good future God has in store for you. You might begin by praying, "God, by the power of the Holy Spirit, I choose to pull down the stronghold of depression that is imprisoning me and replace it with a spirit of joy."

Replace your negative thoughts by filling your mind with uplifting scripture like Psalm 100: 1-5: "Shout for joy to the Lord, all the earth. Worship the Lord with gladness; come before Him with joyful songs. Know that the Lord is God. It is He who made us and we are His; we are His people, the sheep of His pasture. Enter His gates with thanksgiving and His courts with praise; give thanks to Him and praise His name. For the Lord is good and His love endures forever; His faithfulness continues through all generations" (NIV).

Here is another: "Praise the Lord, O my soul; all my innermost being, praise His holy name. Praise the Lord, O my soul and forget not all His benefits. He forgives all my sins and heals all my diseases; He redeems my life from the pit and crowns me with love and compassion. He satisfies my desires with good things so that my youth is renewed like the eagle's" (Psalm 103:1-5, NIV).

To experience peace and joy, realize and acknowledge God's love for you and accept yourself as being special to God. We've spoken elsewhere about this, but the truth bears repeating: we are God's special creations. As Genesis 1:26, 27 puts it, "Then God said, 'Let us make man in Our image, in Our likeness, and let them rule over the fish of the sea and the birds of the air, over the livestock, over all the earth and over all the creatures that move along the earth.' So God created man in His Own image, and in the image of God He created him; male and female He created them" (NIV).

God is able to solve your problems. God has provided the answer for us in the person of Jesus Christ who offers the familiar invitation in Matt 11:28-30, "Come to Me, all you who labor and are heavy laden, and I will give you rest. Take My yoke upon you and learn from Me, for I am gentle and lowly in heart, and you will find rest for your souls. For My yoke is easy and My burden is light."

Other powerful verses to fill your mind include:

"You will keep in perfect peace him whose mind is steadfast, because he trusts in You" (Isaiah 26:3, NIV).

In Isaiah we read, "He gives power to the weak, and to those who have no might He increases strength. Even the youths shall faint and be weary, and the young men shall utterly fall, But those who wait on the LORD shall renew their strength; They shall mount up with wings like eagles, They shall run and not be weary, They shall walk and not faint" (Isaiah 40:29-31).

Perhaps you are saying, "I'd like to believe this is available to me, but God seems so far away." Could it be that you have never personally welcomed God's Son, the Lord Jesus Christ, into your life? It is only by accepting Jesus Christ that you can have rest and peace. God's plan and purpose is for Christ to live in your heart and life, but in order for that to happen, you have to invite Jesus in. You can do that by praying something like this:

"Dear God, I recognize that I can't get rid of depression by myself; I need Your help. I also understand that I cannot get to know You in a personal way unless I know Your Son, Jesus Christ. Therefore, Lord Jesus, I invite You to come into my life, to forgive my sins, and to help me be the person You want me to be. Thank you."

Now, lean heavily on Him. Believe what the Apostle Paul said in Philippians 4:13 and 19: "I can do everything through Him who gives me strength...And my God will meet all your needs according to His glorious riches in Christ Jesus" (NIV). Choose to accept God's forgiveness for your sins. When you have accepted Christ into your life, you then need to believe that God has removed your sins and your guilt.

Your next step is to choose to forgive yourself and others. Because God has forgiven you, you need to forgive yourself and stop condemning yourself. The scripture basis for this is Romans 8:1, 2: "There is therefore now no condemnation to those who are in Christ Jesus, who do not walk according to the flesh, but according to the Spirit." Tell yourself as many times as you need to, "God has forgiven me, now I forgive myself." You also need to forgive others. There is a direct correlation between depression and unwillingness to forgive, and we need to seek God's help in this regard. Forgiving someone is a deliberate choice. If you are not willing to forgive others, you can expect your unforgiveness to manifest itself in ongoing feelings of hurt, retaliation, bitterness, revenge, hostility and rejection.

As quickly as you can, and for the long-term, work on a daily spiritual life. One of the greatest sources of strength in overcoming depression is a daily quiet time during which you read the Bible and meditate on its words. "For the Word of God is living and active," Hebrews 4:12 says, "sharper than any double-edged sword, it penetrates even to dividing soul and spirit, joints and marrow; it judges the thoughts and attitudes of the heart" (NIV).

God's Word impacts us emotionally, spiritually, physically, mentally and socially. Studying the Word of God together with other believers, sharing joys and problems, and praying together will mature you as a Christian. "Let the Word of Christ dwell in you richly as you teach and admonish one another with all wisdom and as you sing psalms, hymns and spiritual songs with gratitude in your hearts to God" (Colossians 3:16, NIV). Paul states in Ephesians, "And do not be drunk with wine, in which is dissipation; but be filled with the spirit, speaking to one another in psalms and hymns and spiritual songs, singing and making melody in your heart to the Lord, giving thanks always for all things to God the Father in the name of our Lord Jesus Christ, submitting to one another in the fear of God" (Ephesians 5: 18-21).

Remember, you can talk (pray) to God the Father, asking Him for guidance in your life. Stay in close communication with God who loves you and wants you to walk in obedience to Him. Christ will enable you to do this. Claim this promise: "If you remain in me and my words remain in you, ask whatever you wish and it will be given you" (John 15:7, NIV).

If you are chronically depressed, you need to consider the possibility that medical problems are involved. If you even suspect there might be a medical cause for your depression, be sure to check it out immediately with a competent medical doctor.

Continue Your Victory Over Depression

1. Ask God to fill you with his Holy Spirit. Renew your relationship with God daily through prayer and Bible study.
2. Seek the Kingdom of God. "But seek first His kingdom and His righteousness, and all these things will be given to you as well" (Matthew 6:33, NIV).
3. Choose to memorize scripture and quote the verses to yourself out loud.
4. Accept God's forgiveness for your sins.

   "If we confess our sins, He is faithful and just to forgive us our sins and to cleanse us from all unrighteousness" (1 John 1:9).
5. Accept yourself as special to God. Renew your relationship with yourself by studying yourself, pinpointing your strengths and weaknesses. Establish your priorities. By faith, visualize and write down your basic life goals. Build your self-esteem by reading and memorizing God's Word.
6. Give yourself to God to serve other people.
7. Cultivate a spirit of thankfulness. "Rejoice always, pray without ceasing, in everything give thanks; for this is the will of God in Christ Jesus for you" (1 Thessalonians 5:16-18).

   "But thanks be to God! He gives us the victory through our Lord Jesus Christ" (1 Corinthians 15:57, NIV). Psalm 37 also gives us instruction regarding what we need to do to tap into the help God desires to give us. In the psalm we read phrases like "Trust in the Lord," "Be delighted in God," "Commit your way to God," and "Rest in the Lord."

My today commitments

For continued victory over depression, make these your homework, daily commitments to keep you on the right track.

- Today, I will praise the Lord for who He is. And who is the Lord? According to Psalm 24:1, "The earth is the Lord's and everything in it, the world, and all who live in it" (NIV). This is further substantiated by Psalm 100: 1-5: "Shout for joy to the Lord, all the earth. Worship the Lord with gladness; come before Him with joyful songs. Know that the Lord is God. It is He who made us and we are His; we are His people, the sheep of His pasture. Enter His gates with thanksgiving and His courts with praise; give thanks to Him and praise His name. For the Lord is good and His love endures forever; His faithfulness continues through all generations" (NIV), "Praise the Lord, O my soul; all my inmost being, praise His holy name. Praise the Lord, O my soul, and forget not all His benefits—who forgives all your sins and heals all your diseases, who redeems your life from the pit and crowns you with love and compassion, who satisfies your desires with good things, so that your youth is renewed like the eagle's" (Psalm 103:1-5, NIV).
- Today, I will submit myself to God's will for my life regardless of the situation I find myself in. "And we know that in all things God works for the good of those who love him, who have been called according to His purpose" (Romans 8:28, NIV).

"Submit yourselves, then, to God. Resist the devil and he will flee from you" (James 4:7, NIV).

- Today, I will give attention to reading God's Word and applying the Biblical principles to my life. "For the Word of God is alive and active. Sharper than any double-edged sword, it penetrates even to dividing soul and spirit, joints and marrow; it judges the thoughts and attitudes of the heart" (Hebrews 4:12, NIV). "I have hidden Your word in my heart that I might not sin against You" (Psalm 119:11, NIV).
- Today, I will allow Jesus Christ to control every area of my life and be Lord in my life.

"That at the name of Jesus every knee should bow, in heaven and on earth and under the earth, and every tongue confess that Jesus Christ is Lord, to the glory of God the Father" (Philippians 2:10, 11, NIV).

- Today, I will not give in to Satan's attacks. Rather, I will call on the name of Jesus Christ, claim the blood of Jesus Christ, and the work of Jesus Christ to win every battle. "Finally, be strong in the Lord and in His mighty power. Put on the full armor of God so that you can take your stand against the Devil's schemes. For our struggle is not against flesh and blood, but against the rulers, against the authorities, against the powers of this dark world and against the spiritual forces of evil in the heavenly realms. Therefore put on the full armor of God, so that when the day of evil comes, you may be able to stand your ground and after you have done everything, to stand. Stand firm then, with the belt of truth buckled around your waist, with the breastplate of righteousness in place, and with your feet fitted with the readiness that comes from the gospel of peace. In addition to all this, take up the shield of faith, with which you can extinguish all the flaming arrows of the evil one. Take the helmet of salvation and the sword of the Spirit, which is the Word of God. And pray in the Spirit on all occasions with all kinds of prayers and requests. With this in mind, be alert and always keep on praying for all the saints" (Ephesians 6: 10-18, NIV). "And do not give the devil a foothold"(Ephesians 4:27).

"They overcame him by the blood of the Lamb and by the word of their testimony; they did not love their lives so much as to shrink from death"(Revelation 12:11, NIV).

- Today, I will not give in to negative thoughts, anger, and self-pity, failures of the past or fears of the future. "Rejoice in the Lord always. I will say it again: Rejoice! Let your gentleness be evident to all. The Lord is near. Do not be anxious about anything, but in every situation, by prayer and petition, with thanksgiving, present your requests to God. And the peace of God, which transcends all understanding, will guard your hearts and your minds in Christ Jesus. Finally brothers and sisters, whatever is true; whatever is noble; whatever is right, whatever is pure, whatever is lovely, whatever is admirable—if anything is excellent or praiseworthy—think about such things" (Philippians 4:4-8, NIV).

• Today, I will call out to God when I am distressed. Even if you don't have all the words to describe your distress, tell God how you're feeling. He already knows your situation and state and He cares. Ask Bible-believing people to pray with you and for you. That might be all you can do for a while, but God promises He will "make a way for you in the desert place." Ask God to bring the right people to you for support. But even if you don't know anyone who can pray with you and for you, here are some prayers that you can pray yourself: "Lord, I thank You that You hear my cry no matter what my circumstances are or what I've done. You know I have trouble in my life. Please come and save me. Please bring me out of this darkness and deep gloom." Remember, "The Lord is close to the brokenhearted and saves those who are crushed in spirit" (Psalm 34:18).

Or you might pray: "Lord, my heart is broken, and there are people I love who are experiencing the same thing. There is so much in our world that crushes us to the point of despair. Thank you that You promise to be close during these times. Today, I ask for Your closeness. The Bible says if we draw near to You, You will draw near to us. I do this right now, and I accept Your comfort."

You may be thinking, why pray? What will it do for me? After all, I'm just saying words. You might just be saying the words, but you're saying them to the One who is Hope—Jesus Christ, the Son of God, who chose to do for you what you could not do for yourself. Jesus is not some dead figure in ancient history; He is alive. He is there for anyone who turns to Him. And He offers the gift of eternal life to everyone who believes in Him. Jesus said, "For God so loved the world that He gave His one and only Son that whoever believes in Him will not perish but will have eternal life" (John 3:16).

We cannot save ourselves from depression, or sadness, or from any feelings of futility and loneliness. We cannot give ourselves hope. But Jesus can. That's because Jesus is hope—the hope of eternal life, the hope of a meaningful life today, and the assurance that in Him—the Prince of Peace—alone, we will experience true and enduring peace.

This hope is found when you put your faith in Jesus Christ, when you acknowledge that you have sinned, and when you ask for His forgiveness. Then you must trust Him to give you a life-changing relationship with God who has promised to forgive you and give you a new heart to love and trust Him. God promises never to leave you or abandon you.

I found the following text on a Dayspring card. Though I don't know who wrote it, it is based on 1 Corinthians 15:57:

"When you are the neediest, He is the most sufficient.
When you are completely helpless, He is the most helpful.
When you feel totally dependent, He is absolutely dependable.
When you are the weakest, He is the most able.
When you are the most alone, He is intimately present.
When you feel you are the least, He is the greatest.
When you feel the most useless, He is preparing you.
When it is the darkest, He is the only light you need.
When you feel the least secure, He is your rock and your fortress."

—Anonymous

Jesus Christ will always respond to the deepest cries of your heart. In your depression, you can turn to Him in prayer anytime, anywhere, with the questions that fill your mind.

He hears.
He listens.
He understands.
He will give you real hope.

CHAPTER 9: SAYING GOODBYE: DEATH AND GRIEF

In our home it is not unusual to receive a phone call from individuals who are hurting, overwhelmed with emotional pain and desperately trying to cope with their brokenness and loss. This phone call was different. It affected me so personally that tears came to my eyes and I struggled to speak. My special friend and prayer partner, Ron, had just shared that their 24-year-old daughter had passed away with a blood clot in her lung. Ron wanted me to take her funeral. Amanda had been like another daughter to us, so I realized that this would be a difficult ministry for me.

Although she would not have known it at the time, Amanda had prepared me for the meditation at the memorial service. Her spiritual insights that were recorded in her journal brought incredible peace to all of us as I read some of her special, personal notations. It was so obvious to all the believers in the service that Amanda had an exceptional relationship with her Lord and Saviour Jesus Christ and even at that moment, she was enjoying His wonderful presence.

The next morning Ron knew that the Lord was compelling them to read God's Word and to simply listen. The days, weeks and months following were filled with extreme pain and loss, but Ron and Gladys determined that they would remain in God's Word and discover that Christ, Himself, became their Answer and their Life. They are convinced that the gospel of Christ is true and that one day they will enjoy their reunion with Christ and Amanda.

With any death there are many questions and few answers. I remember one particular young man who took his own life. Seeing him lying in a casket was a wretched, sobering experience. Knowing he was there because he committed suicide made it almost overwhelming. Even more devastating was the fact that this young man was my son's classmate. What would cause a young, energetic, athletic teenager to end his life with a squeeze of the trigger on a high-powered rifle? Why didn't he call for help? Did those around him not see his turmoil, or hear his silent call for help?

Another young woman was at the top of her class: a leader, a happy-go-lucky young woman with tons of potential. So why did she slip into her parents' garage, start the engine of the car, roll down the windows, and allow carbon monoxide to fill her lungs? Not only was a life destroyed, family members were overwhelmed with grief and a profound sense of guilt because they were not able to prevent this tragedy.

To lose one son to suicide is devastating, but to lose two sons to suicide within a ten-year period is life-shattering. That was the painful story of a woman who wept uncontrollably in my counseling office. Not only was her own grief overwhelming, but her husband—the father of these two precious young men—refused to discuss with her why these tragedies could possibly have occurred. He had work to do and wasn't interested in dialoguing about his two sons who he felt weren't strong enough to win at life.

Understandably, suicide is one of the most difficult types of grief to overcome. Every anniversary of the death, every birthday, every special holiday is a painful reminder that the loved one is missing, and the awful circumstances that took them away.

Fifteen out of every 100,000 Canadians die each year by suicide. According to the Center for Disease Control and Prevention, the number of suicides in the United States is just slightly lower: 12 in every 100,000. Men commit suicide at a rate four times higher than the rate for women. In fact, statistics from the Canadian Institute for Health Information show that more men in Ontario commit suicide than die in car crashes. Suicide accounts for nearly one-quarter of all deaths in

North America among 15 to 24 year-olds, and 16% among 16 to 44 year-olds. The suicide rate for Inuit youth is a shocking eleven times the national average.

The common perception that suicide rates are highest during the Christmas season is not true, though studies show that depression increases significantly during that time. Most suicides occur in late July and August. Some suggest the increase may be due to seasonal change and changes in personal situations. It is definitely a high-risk time for teens going back to school. There is also a significant correlation between a history of sexual abuse and suicide attempts. The correlation is twice as strong for women as for men. Suffice it to say, suicide is one of the top ten leading causes of death in North America, and rates have been steadily increasing over the past 65 years.

Reports of suicide have become so commonplace we hardly pay attention to them anymore. Many movie stars—who one might think have everything in the world going for them—find life so empty and meaningless that they end it.

At the age of 65, author Ernest Hemingway supposedly had it all, yet he put a gun to his head and ended his life. The note he left behind read: "Life is one damn thing after another."

Why would someone like Hemingway, who appeared to have everything going for him, do that? There is a perception that those at the top of the ladder financially, professionally, academically, or socially have all the answers, yet statistics suggest that—compared to the rest of the population—the highest suicide rates occur among psychiatrists, law enforcement officers and lawyers.

Why, we ask, do people destroy themselves? The key reasons for suicide are emptiness within and pressures without. Fear, guilt, loss of a loved one, depression, bitterness, hatred and low self-esteem (many of the negative emotions we have already dealt with in this book) have all been known to trigger suicide. If individuals do not have their needs met they may resort to suicide. Young people, in particular, find themselves with their backs to the wall. They have no answers to life and struggle within themselves. Suicide seems the only way to end the struggle.

Warning Signs of Suicide

According to noted Christian psychologists, counselors and psychiatrists, there are a number of warning signs and conditions under which suicide is predictable. If a number of these are exhibited together, be on guard:

- intense emotional pain or depression.
- intense feelings of hopelessness.
- a prior history of suicide.
- voiced warnings of suicide intentions.
- forming a plan. (I have worked with clients who talked about getting into the bathtub, breaking a light bulb, sticking the cord in the water and "frying themselves." Others planned to use guns, knives, or sleeping pills.)
- self-destructive behaviours like eating disorders or an intense need to achieve.
- death of a spouse or friend, loss of a job, or some other disturbing life event within the previous six months.
- drastic change in behaviour—from continual depression to extreme joy, for instance, or withdrawal.
- loss of sleep or extreme fatigue.
- decline in work productivity.
- an increase in smoking, drinking, or drug use.
- giving away possessions with statements like, "I won't need this anymore."
- themes of death described through art, poetry, or music.

None of these signs should be taken lightly; any one of them could be a cry for help. We need to be alert and ready to respond. If you or someone you know is thinking about suicide because there seems to be no other alternative, please know this: **There is an alternative.** There are steps you can take that will bring freedom from this destructive desire to end your life, and lasting victory for this life and for eternity.

Steps to Freedom

Realize that you are a Very Important Person—a person of great worth. You are not on planet Earth just because of a chance biological union between a man and a woman. You are a uniquely designed human being created by a loving God. King David said hundreds of years ago, "You [God] have formed my inward parts; You have [woven] me in my mother's womb. I will praise You, for I am fearfully and wonderfully made...My frame was not hidden from You...Your eyes saw my substance, being yet unformed. And in Your book they all were written, the days fashioned for me when as yet there were none of them. . . ."(Psalm 139:13-16).

God makes this astonishing statement in Genesis 1:26, 27: ". . . let Us make man in Our image, according to Our likeness. . . . So God created man in His own image; in the image of God He created him; male and female He created them." It is obvious that to design us after His own image, God views us being very special, indeed.

Realize that this physical life is only the beginning. In the book of Job we read, "If a man dies, shall he live again?" (Job 14:14). The Apostle Paul said, "There will be a resurrection of the dead, both of the just and the unjust" (Acts 24:15). The writer of Hebrews declared: "It is appointed for men to die once, but **after** this the judgement" (Hebrews 9:27). Neither suicide nor death by any other means is the end of existence.

Realize that you have an enemy whom the Bible calls Satan or the Devil. He is described in 1 Peter 5:8 as a "roaring lion, seeking whom he may devour." Hebrews 2:14 tells us that the Devil "had the power of death." Satan's cohorts are demons or unclean spirits. In Mark 9 we read about a man's son who was demon-possessed. In verse 22 the boy's father recounts how "often [the unclean spirit] has thrown him both into the fire and into the water to destroy him!" Consider that Satan may be trying to destroy **you** by means of suicide.

Know that Jesus Christ can save you from suicide and give you freedom from guilt.

Jesus said in John 11:25, "...I am the resurrection and the life. He who **believes** in Me, though he may die [physically], he shall live [eternally with God]." In Hebrews 2:14 we learn that Christ's death on the cross destroyed the power of the Devil who had authority over death. "For God so loved the world that He gave his only begotten Son, that whoever **believes** in Him should not perish but have everlasting life" (John 3:16).

The Lord Jesus invites you to receive Him into your heart and life. Revelation 3:20 says, "Behold, I stand at the door [of your heart] and knock. If anyone hears My voice and opens the door, I will come in to him and dine with him, and he with Me." And consider this verse: "But as many as received Him, to them He gave the right to become children of God, even to those who believe in His name" (John 1:12).

Perhaps you have thought of committing suicide. You don't have to, because Jesus Christ can transform this life you hate and make you a new creation.

When you are the person grieving a sudden death

"There are always two parties to a death," said historian Arnold Toynbee, "...the person who dies and the survivors who are bereaved...and in the apportionment of suffering, the survivor takes the brunt."

One of the most powerful stories of freedom from grief after the death of a loved one comes from Victoria Cummock, an American woman whose husband John was murdered along with 269 other people on Pan Am Flight 103. Because of a terrorist's bomb, Pan Am Flight 103 exploded over Lockerbie, Scotland, on December 21, 1988, killing everyone aboard. Victoria Cummock was left a widow with three children under the age of six.

Victoria's story is told in Kenneth Doka's book *Living With Grief After Sudden Loss: Suicide, Homicide, Accident, Heart Attack, Stroke.* (©1996, Hospice Foundation of America. Reprinted with permission.)

It was a tragic day for Victoria and her children. In that instant, she said, she lost a loving partner, a wonderful marriage, and the economic security of a two-income household. The reality also hit her that she would have to raise her three small children without John.

According to Victoria, the journey through grief took many years for each member of the family. There were times when she felt she was going insane. Searing anguish and mental fragmentation overwhelmed her as she struggled with the loss of her husband. She had trouble eating, and difficulty relating. Statements people made regarding her loss hurt more than they helped.

"I found no consolation in hearing, 'You're young...you'll find another husband,'" she said. "Instead, my anger rose. I didn't want to hear things like that. I'd lost my best friend and my husband. I wanted him back."

Other people offered her jobs so she could 'keep busy and not have to deal with the trauma.' But Victoria realized she needed time to grieve. She needed to find consolation and comfort on her own.

During her time of grief, a wise therapist encouraged Victoria to feel her feelings, to accept that grieving is hard work and realize there is no precise timing for the healing process. Victoria needed to recognize that losing a husband and father, as she and her children had, would be a lifelong difficulty.

Part of her healing began when Victoria realized that although she didn't have a choice in what happened to John, she did have a choice about its impact on her. She determined not to let the terrorists ruin everyone else's life as well as take the life of her husband. Victoria learned that a number of the families who experienced the murder of their loved one in the same Pan Am Flight 103 disaster refused professional and mental health counseling. These people had a long, tough struggle with the painful issues of grief, especially anger. Seven years after the incident, they were still stuck in their grief because they had not dealt with the loss, and therefore had not been able to move on with their lives.

Perhaps the greatest difficulty for grieving individuals in these circumstances is that they do not have a chance to see the body of their loved one.

Death of any kind without forewarning always creates problems for survivors. As a counselor, I know that these losses affect every area of a person's life.

Because we human beings are not made up of just one part, I see the impact of pain and loss as five-fold: emotional, physical, mental, social and spiritual. Every one of these areas is affected when a friend or a loved one dies.

During a seminar on death and dying, a gentleman in the audience asked if he might speak with me privately. The man was a pastor who had lost several family members in a tragic accident. His loss was immense; he was totally devastated. Yet after a very short time, one of his parishioners came to him and said, "Pastor, you've grieved long enough.

It's time to get back to work." The man was deeply hurt by the insensitive remark, and horrified to think that one in his congregation would
make a statement like that. I assured this man that grieving takes a long
time, and the closer we were to the individual who passed away, the
longer it takes and the harder we have to work to find healing. Further,
we need to realize that not every person, or every age group, will grieve
in the same way.

Children and Grieving

In his book, *A Child's View of Grief*, Dr. Alan D. Wolfelt, the director
of the Center for Loss and Life Transitions, writes that adults should
never assume they know exactly how children feel emotionally and
how they react when a loved one dies. According to Wolfelt, there are
several predictable dimensions to childhood grief:

1. Apparent Lack of Feelings

Children will often respond to the death of a loved one with emotional
shock that may be manifest as an apparent lack of feelings. The child can
be playing in the yard only hours or even minutes after learning of the
death. This is a protective mechanism that allows the child detachment
from the pain in the only way available. Adults need to be supportive
and accept this as a necessary step toward healing.

2. Regressive Behaviour

This usually occurs immediately after the death. Under the normal
stress of grief, children will often return to what gave them a sense
of security in former times. There may be a need to be close to, or
be rocked by a parent or grandparent. The child may demand constant
attention, or express fear of the dark. Fortunately, regressive behaviour is
generally temporary.

3. Big-Man/Big-Woman Syndrome

This is apparent when the child tries to grow up quickly in an effort
to replace the one who has died. Sometimes this behaviour results from
some adult saying, "You'll have to be the man/woman of the house
now." This suddenly enforced maturity can result in a frustrated or

depressed child because they have not been allowed to grieve in ways that are appropriate to their age. Even more damaging are situations where grieving adults allow children to become emotional replacements for a dead spouse.

4. Explosive Emotions

This is the most upsetting dimension of juvenile grieving. Underlying it is the child's primary feelings of pain, helplessness, frustration and rage. It is natural for a grieving child to be angry, and that anger may be directed toward any available person: a surviving parent, a teacher, a friend, God, or the world in general. Explosive emotions are actually healthy because they are a means of temporarily protesting the painful reality of the loss.

5. Acting-out

Acting-out in grief may be demonstrated by temper outbursts, becoming unusually loud, initiating fights, defying authority, and rebelling against everyone. Sometimes there is a drop in grades, or an 'I don't care' attitude. Older adolescents may talk about running away from home. When any of these behaviours is exhibited, parents need to examine the cause. Are there feelings of insecurity? Feelings of abandonment? A desire to provoke punishment "because they deserve to be punished"? A desire to protect themselves against future loss by refusing to get too close to another person?

Acting-out is generally an externalizing of feelings of grief—a way of saying, "I hurt, too."

6. Loss and Loneliness

For a child, feelings of loss and loneliness rarely come immediately after the death. It may be several weeks or months before the child finally comes to grips with the reality that the missing person is never coming back. The realization may bring on depression, but this, too, is a natural response to the loss.

7. Reconciliation

This is the final dimension of healthy grief. And while children never get over the loss, they can become reconciled to it. They come to recognize that life will be different without the person who is missing, yet they have a renewed desire to once again be involved in life. Adults need to listen carefully to what the child is saying, and provide love, support, and understanding.

Adolescent Grieving

Given their age and activities, teenagers generally have many more opportunities to experience the death of someone they love than do children. But because adolescence is already so fraught with chaos, the death of someone close is all the more devastating. The grieving young person may experience significant psychological, physiological and academic difficulties.

The messages grieving young people are given are often unhealthy: "Keep your chin up," "Be strong," "Keep busy." The truth is, repression of grief only leads to anger, sadness and isolation.

The process of adolescent mourning is a naturally complicated experience. It is imperative that caring adults be supportive and understanding during this time.

Adults and Grieving

For adults, the death of a loved one isn't the only circumstance that generates grief. Abuse, bankruptcy, divorce, abortion/miscarriage, long-term illness, ongoing work pressures, decisions that go sour, children leaving home, financial losses, retirement—they can all have long-term negative effects on the sufferer. The grieving person may experience lack of energy, crying jags, temper outbursts, constant worry, loneliness, and a sense of being ignored. There may be feelings of persecution, entrapment, hopelessness regarding the future, worthlessness, an inability to concentrate, or worry that one's mind is failing. There is little excitement about anything and a tendency toward a sloppy and careless demeanour. You can't pray or meditate; you feel God has abandoned you.

As we look at death, separation and loss, it is important to realize that every person is special and unique, and that the process, duration, and intensity of grieving—and spiritual healing—will be different for each one who suffers. There are, however, a number of predictable aspects to grieving that will most likely be common to all.

Shock and denial are a common part of grief for those who have lost a loved one. Denial of reality is a normal defence mechanism that we use to shield ourselves from unpleasant realities such as death. In denial, we refuse to fully perceive or face what has happened.

Healthy grieving includes expressing emotion by crying. I often hear people saying, "I lost my loved one and I don't think I'll ever stop crying." Crying is therapeutic and helpful for both men and women in dealing with the loss of a loved one.

In the process of grief we may feel depressed and lonely. Depression often goes hand in hand with emotional loss. Extended depression, however, can sink the grieving person into a state of helplessness and hopelessness.

The grieving person may experience physical symptoms. I remind people who have experienced a significant loss that they shouldn't be surprised if they suddenly begin to experience physical complaints. That's because the stress of grief and the stress of rethinking the pain of the loss can give rise to physical symptoms.

Some grieving individuals may feel panicky or out of control, as if they are unable to get a grip on life. This, too, is a normal part of the process of grief. There may also be feelings of guilt: Why couldn't I have prevented the death of my husband? my child? my wife? If only I had done (or hadn't done) this, or that. . . but in reality, there was probably nothing you could have done to make the outcome different.

It is important to remember that there are two kinds of guilt: real guilt and false guilt. With the loss of a loved one, there is almost always some false guilt involved. This kind of guilt comes from the world or from others who would address your situation in a condemning way: "You should have called the doctor sooner," or "You shouldn't have allowed your teenager to run with those people." Do not own or internalize these expressions of false guilt. The "flesh," or our natural human tendency, is another source of false guilt. It occurs when the grieving person is inundated by the pressure of self-imposed guilt because of what happened.

I remember a father who had a special game he played with his little boy. When the dad came home from work, he would honk the horn when he got to the driveway. The little boy would run outside, jump in the car, and the two would roar into the garage. One day the dad honked and honked and honked, but the boy didn't appear. Thinking his little son must be busy doing something inside, the dad drove into the garage—just as the little boy jumped out in front of the car and yelled, "Boo, Daddy!" The car struck and killed the boy. Devastated by guilt, the grieving father needed help to find healing.

Satan is the third source of false guilt. He will tell you that God is punishing you, that you deserve what happened because you're bad, anyway. The only One who reveals *true guilt* is God's Holy Spirit. Jesus said the Holy Spirit would guide us into all truth, that the Holy Spirit comes and convicts the world of sin. Real guilt is conviction from the Holy Spirit when we have sinned. The Spirit tells us when we need to deal with the sin in our life.

Feelings of anger, hostility, and resentment may also come immediately following the loss, or even later. The pastor who was told he had grieved enough felt angry because he had not had the opportunity to work through even the initial stages of grief before being forced back to work.

Victoria Cummock admitted to feeling extremely angry and resentful. One reason for her frustration was her inability to get answers, when all she asked was for people to be honest with her about what really happened.

Anger and hostility may appear in four areas:

1. We are angry at ourselves because we were unable to prevent the tragedy. Sometimes the anger and self-loathing can be so intense that watches need to be put on the individuals to prevent them from harming themselves. I see this often when dealing with adolescents who feel the need to punish themselves because they couldn't control what happened (especially if they had something to do with the tragedy).

2. We are angry at God. People often blame God for what has happened. In my counseling work over the years, I have worked with many, many people who are angry at God. "Why did God allow this?" they wonder. "Why didn't God prevent that death? Where was He, anyway?"

3. We are angry at friends. In our grief, we may feel hostile toward even those who are trying to show love and help us. We need to be aware that even good and loving friends do not always use appropriate verses or statements in their attempts to bring comfort. Romans 8:28, for instance, is often used inappropriately. It says, "And we know that all things work together for good for those who love God, to those who are the called according to His [God's] purpose." To hear that verse recited just hours or days after losing a loved one can cause much emotional damage for the grieving person.

4. We are angry at the one who has left, whether through divorce, separation, death, or a mental condition. Some individuals become so angry at the circumstance, their anger becomes an emotional prison (or stronghold) from which they cannot escape. It may take them years to get over the loss. They may even go to their grave without being healed.

The inability to return to usual or "normal" activities is another reality in the process of grieving. There is a tendency to withdraw into passivity in order to protect ourselves from further hurt. Like a child's grief, we may even regress or retreat to earlier developmental stages involving less mature responses and a lower level of aspiration. The individual who has had a high position in a company, for instance, may choose to take a lesser job just so he won't have to cope with the pressure of carrying on.

The struggle to affirm reality is another common aspect of grieving. I have worked with clients who just couldn't cope with what was going on around them. They had lost their perspective of night and day, of looking after themselves. Their job had no meaning. Looking after the children alone had no meaning. Making money had no meaning. Maintaining a quality of life had no meaning. Interacting with others had no meaning.

Thankfully, in the natural process of grief, hope gradually comes through. Because grief affects so many areas of life, it may take a long time for hope to surface. The saddest part is that many individuals hold in their grief, and do not allow themselves to move through the natural grieving process. When that happens, they are unable to move on in their life to freedom.

Key to grieving—and usually coming at the very end of the grieving process—is sharing memories of the loved one.

Make an effort to tell people how special that person was, and the positive and enduring things you remember about them. This will help you on your way to spiritual healing and growth through one of life's saddest times.

How Can We Best Cope With Loss?

Shifting our focus away from the loss, disappointment, grief, or hurt can help us. I encourage people to go for help to someone who already understands the grieving process.

If our hearts are crushed and filled with disbelief, panic, anger and fear (normal reactions to loss), we need to identify the painful thoughts and feelings. We need to realize that God loves us and understands our hurts.

If we are partly responsible for the pain and loss, we must ask for and choose to accept God's forgiveness. We also need to forgive others who have caused the pain and loss. Those who refuse to do so have a much harder time getting past their grief.

Not everyone knows how to respond to someone in grief, therefore, we need to be on guard against unkind words or actions from thought-less people, and be wary regarding the lies the Enemy (Satan) would tell us.

Paramount to spiritual healing and growth through grief is living a daily spiritual life, reading the Bible, being obedient to the Word, and having a regular time of prayer. During this process, we become aware that negative emotions from hurt and loss can lead to depression. Depression can also come from pain that is not dealt with.) Refer back to Chapter 8 on depression to remind yourself how best to cope—and even flourish—while making your way through depression.

Those who grieve need to acknowledge that life will never be exactly the same as it was before, and choose to walk in the new reality with the Shepherd. I encourage grieving people to take comfort and direction from Psalm 23, particularly verses 4 to 6: "Yea, though I walk through the valley of the shadow of death, I will fear no evil, for You are with me; Your rod and Your staff, they comfort me. You prepare a table before me in the presence of my enemies; You anoint my head with oil; my cup runs over. Surely goodness and mercy shall follow me all the days of my life and I will dwell in the house of the Lord forever."

I like the refrain of "Blessed Quietness" an old gospel song by Marie P. Ferguson:

"Blessed quietness, holy quietness, What assurance in my soul, On the stormy sea Jesus speaks peace to me as the billows cease to roll." If you enjoy YouTube, you can watch a video of this song being performed.

Normal Grieving

Clients sometimes ask me, "What does normal grieving look like, and how long does it take?" Though everyone grieves differently, all the grieving we've talked about in this chapter is normal, and all grieving people have common needs. These needs are love and concern, and someone to reach out and help them. They also need spiritual and emotional help to find healing.

I encourage those who are grieving to implement the following suggestions:

- Do not totally withdraw from life.
- Do not deny what you're feeling: your anger, fear, and disappointment. If you do, the healing process will take a lot longer. Be ready to admit to God, or to a friend: "I'm hurting. That's how I feel right now."
- Do not put yourself down for feeling weak and vulnerable. Criticizing yourself is destructive and unproductive, not helpful.
- Do not dwell on the unfairness of it all.
- Do not jump into a new relationship to try to cover or avoid the pain. Being with someone else too quickly will not satisfy the sense of loss, and will only prolong the healing.
- Do not be surprised if you develop some physical complaints. These are a common result of the stress or pressure you're going through.

Those walking alongside grieving people need to let them know that victory is possible. God is there in every situation, and in our grief. Romans 8:37-39 reminds us: "Yet in all these things, we are more than conquerors through Him who loved us. For I am persuaded that neither death nor life, nor angels nor principalities nor powers, nor things present nor things to come, nor height nor depth, nor any other created thing, shall be able to separate us from the love of God which is in Christ Jesus our Lord."

Spiritual and Emotional Help for the Hurting

Here are ten things you can do to begin healing. They are a compilation of ideas from other care workers as well as my own observations as I deal with grieving individuals.

1. **Aim at your own goals.** People can be unkind in their statements and because we're vulnerable in our grief, we try to follow their advice instead of what we know to be best for us.
2. **Realize that the healing process takes a long time**, and that special holidays like Christmas, anniversaries, graduations, or birthdays will spark old memories.
3. In your desire to speed the healing process, **remember that trying to force it may result in frustration of the spirit**. Believe that time and God's ministry within you will eventually lessen the pain.
4. **Make decisions one at a time**, and don't try to do everything all at once.
5. Find a way to **ask for help.**
6. **Work on a regular routine**. Some people have a hard time going back to work following a difficult experience.
7. **Eat regularly.** After a tragedy, most people don't feel like eating.

---

8. Get out and **exercise.**
9. **Say no** to those who would contradict or criticize how you're feeling.
10. **Lean heavily** on God. "Have you not known? Have you not heard? The everlasting God, the Lord, the Creator of the ends of the earth, neither faints nor is weary. His understanding is unsearchable. He gives power to the weak; and to those who have no might He increases strength. Even the youths shall faint and be weary, and the young men shall utterly fall. But those who wait on the Lord shall renew their strength; they shall mount up with wings like eagles, they shall run and not be weary, they shall walk and not faint"(Isaiah 40: 28-31).

Those walking alongside grieving people need to let them know that victory is possible. God is there in every situation, and in our grief. Romans 8:37-39 reminds us: "Yet in all these things, we are more than conquerors through Him who loved us. For I am persuaded that neither death nor life, nor angels nor principalities nor powers, nor things present nor things to come, nor height nor depth, nor any other created thing, shall be able to separate us from the love of God which is in Christ Jesus our Lord."

A prayer I find exciting is the prayer of Jabez which is found in 1 Chronicles 4:10: "Oh, that You would bless me indeed, and enlarge my territory, that Your hand would be with me, and that You would keep me from evil, that I may not cause pain!" The Scripture says that God granted Jabez what he requested.

Also helpful and uplifting is Jude 24, 25: "Now to Him who is able to keep you from stumbling, and to present you faultless before the presence of His glory with exceeding joy, to God our Saviour, Who alone is wise, be glory and majesty, dominion and power, both now and forever."

God's Victory Over Pain

Spiritual healing, even in the most difficult times of grief, is a promise given to us by God, and you can be an active participant in that process.

1. As a believer, ask God to fill you with His Spirit. "And do not be drunk with wine, in which is dissipation; but be filled with the Spirit" (Ephesians 5:18).

2. Ask God to show you His will in the midst of this pain and difficulty. "If any of you lacks wisdom, let him ask of God, who gives to all liberally and without reproach, and it will be given to him" (James 1:5).

3. Choose to memorize scripture and quote the verses out loud. "For the word of God is living and powerful, and sharper than any two-edged sword, piercing even to the division of the soul and spirit and of joints and marrow, and is a discerner of the thoughts and intents of the heart" (Hebrews 4:12).

4. Accept God's forgiveness for your sins. "If we confess our sins, He is faithful and just to forgive us our sins and to cleanse us from all unrighteousness" (1 John 1:9).

5. Choose to forgive others who have hurt you. "And be kind to one another, tenderhearted, forgiving one another, even as God in Christ forgave you" (Ephesians 4:32).

6. Forgive yourself and accept yourself as a special person of God. "Then God said, 'Let Us make man in Our image, according to Our likeness; let them have dominion over the fish of the sea, over the birds of the air, and over the cattle, over all the earth and over every creeping thing that creeps on the earth.' So God created man in His own image, in the image of God He created him, male and female He created them" (Genesis 1:26, 27).

7. Give yourself to God to serve people. "For you, brethren, have been called to liberty; only do not use liberty as an opportunity for the flesh, but through love serve one another" (Galatians 5:13).

8. Choose to be thankful. "In everything give thanks, for this is the will of God in Christ Jesus for you" (1 Thessalonians 5:18).

The comfort and healing that God gives to us in our grieving has an added purpose. It enables us to minister to others who are going through similar experiences.

"Blessed be the God and Father of our Lord Jesus Christ, the Father of mercies and God of all comfort, who comforts us in all our tribulation that we may be able to comfort those who are in any trouble with the comfort with which we ourselves are comforted by God" (2 Corinthians 1: 3, 4).

Perhaps one of the most poignant accounts of grief and faith in the face of profound bereavement is found in the life of Joseph Scriven, a poet born in Dublin, Ireland in 1819. Scriven was engaged to be married, but his fiancée accidentally drowned the night before their wedding.

In his profound sadness, Joseph came to Canada where he devoted himself to ministry. He eventually fell in love with a lady named Eliza Rock, but just before they were to be married, she died suddenly of pneumonia. Not long afterward, Scriven received word that his mother in Ireland was gravely ill. Being well-acquainted with grief and loss, he wrote a poem to comfort her. It was titled *Pray Without Ceasing*, but would eventually be put to music under another name, *What A Friend We Have in Jesus*.

The lyrics of that beloved hymn have brought peace to thousands around the world who struggle with pain, loss, and suffering:

"What a friend we have in Jesus,
all our sins and griefs to bear!
What a privilege to carry
everything to God in prayer!
Oh, what peace we often forfeit,
Oh, what needless pain we bear,
All because we do not carry
everything to God in prayer."

Prayer

"My heart has been wounded, broken and dismayed. Some days I can't put a coherent thought into words regarding the devastating void in my life. But You know, Holy and perfect Father. You had to turn Your back on Your Son Jesus—the Lamb of God who takes away the sins of the world. You experienced the agony of separation not only physically, but spiritually, as well, as Jesus assumed culpability for every human creature's sin. You allowed, even sanctioned the great transfer of my sin to Him so I could be forgiven, healed and made whole. You watched from a distance as He suffered a sickening and foul death by torture. You lived the pain, so walk with me as I live mine, for 'You are my shepherd, I shall not be in want. You make me lie down in green pastures, You lead me beside quiet waters, You restore my soul. You guide me in paths of righteousness for Your name's sake. Even though I walk through the valley of the shadow of death, I will fear no evil, for You are with me. Your rod and Your staff, they comfort me' (Psalm 23:1-4)."

Chapter 10: Am I Wearing a Sign *Please Abuse Me*? Trauma and Abuse

Maria was a nurse who had worked on many hospital wards and seen many things, but nothing prepared her for the horrendous vehicle accident she witnessed one evening on her way home from work. Being a nurse, she immediately stopped to help. One of the victims was a little girl. It was several hours before Marie left the scene of the accident. She did everything she knew to do, but the little girl died.

Soon afterward, Maria began seeing images of the child in her mind, especially when she tried to fall asleep at night. She would sit straight up in bed, her heart pounding, sweat dripping down her body. She couldn't get the awful picture out of her mind, nor quell the gut-wrenching sense of being back in that place of devastation and death. Maria began to question her sanity. Why couldn't she shake off these memories and feelings? She was a nurse, after all. She shouldn't be losing sleep and peace of mind. How could Maria react in such an extreme and unusual way when she didn't even know the victims?

Tran Zu came to Canada as a fifteen-year-old refugee from a country where unrest and bloodshed were daily occurrences. Even though he missed his friends and extended family, he was thankful to be in Canada and away from the terror and fear. Initially, he adjusted well, learned the language, and began making friends at school, but about a year after his arrival, Tran Zu began having such vivid nightmares about his country of birth he was afraid to go to sleep. Fear permeated his days and caused him to withdraw from his family and his new friends. He felt a sense of impending doom, and constantly looked over his shoulder for the sinister threat he was unable to identify or describe. Vivid memories of the horrors he had witnessed came back to him more and more often until he grew numb to his surroundings and was unable to live fully in the present.

Marie's and Tran Zu's reactions are not unusual for individuals who have experienced trauma—either a significant single trauma or multiple fear-generating events. Terror and trauma can come from many directions: being involved in or witnessing a vehicle or work accident, a terrifying event, the sudden or tragic loss of a loved one, or sexual or physical abuse. We all have scars. We all have hurts and pain from traumas in our past.

One winter day I was going to visit a sick friend in a rural hospital. As I neared the hospital entrance, I noticed a flurry of activity. Medical personnel were scurrying in every direction because two little girls had just been brought in with severe burns. Their mother was doing some deep-frying and the oil caught fire. She grabbed the pot and ran to the door, intending to toss it out into the snow. Tragically, her two little girls got in the way. The boiling oil splashed all over the children. I knew in an instant they could not possibly emerge from that trauma without being physically and emotionally scarred for life.

Trauma, by definition, is:
1. A serious injury or shock to the body, as from violence or accident,
2. An emotional wound or shock that creates substantial, lasting damage to the psychological development of a person, often leading to neurosis, or
3. An event or situation that causes great distress and disruption.

Post traumatic stress disorder (PTSD)
We hear a lot about Post Traumatic Stress Disorder (PTSD) these days. While it is often associated with military veterans who spend extended periods in combat zones, it can also develop in people who have witnessed or experienced some extremely terrifying or devastating event

that resulted in their feeling overwhelmed, terrorized, or fearing for their life and safety, or that of another.

Symptoms of Post Traumatic Stress Disorder

- feeling numb or detached from the present.
- reliving the experiences (having flashbacks) again and again in one's mind.
- feeling overwhelming terror even during times when there is no obvious threat.
- hyperarousal (the physical body is alert, 'on guard').
- nightmares or sleep terrors.
- difficulty sleeping.
- feeling detached and/or withdrawing from friends and family.
- feelings of impending doom invading daily living.
- difficulties with concentration and memory.

For some people, the symptoms of PTSD become so encompassing that they struggle in their marriage, they have difficulty keeping a job and managing their day-to-day life (parenting, or going to school). If you believe you have PTSD symptoms, please make an appointment with a medical professional or a psychologist who is trained in diagnosing and treating trauma-related concerns.

Family violence and abuse

Years ago, my sister Sharon, who was eight years old, was dropped off at her foster home and unceremoniously left on the back doorstep. She had no idea where any of the rest of us were, or what was going to happen to her. The foster mother took her inside, ordered her to remove her "filthy" coat, and ushered her to a tiny room off the kitchen—a room that would be Sharon's for the next nine years of her life.

Her foster family consisted of a gentle-spirited man, his extremely domineering wife, and a boy two and a half years older than Sharon who had cerebral palsy and a certain degree of brain damage. Terrified and lonely, Sharon couldn't stop crying. Her tears were interpreted as a lack of appreciation for her "good fortune." This initiated a stream of verbal and mental abuse from her foster mother, a stream that would continue unabated until Sharon left that home as a high school graduate.

Sharon learned the hard way how to survive in her foster home. She could not appear upset or unhappy with anything she was expected to do. Even as a little girl, she had to measure her words and actions meticulously in order to avoid being whacked with the broom handle. She was afraid even to sigh or make an innocent comment, or look a certain way, lest it trigger the foster mother's anger. Sharon existed in a relentless state of worry and anxiety. She was constantly reminded of how awful her family was and what terrible people she came from, and how, if she wasn't careful, she would end up just like them.

One of Sharon's friends in the fourth grade was a boy who was in her Sunday school class and happened to walk the same way to school. The two of them enjoyed tramping through the woods, climbing trees, and making up games like the ones we all used to play together. Unfortunately, having a boy for a friend caused problems with her foster mother who often screamed at her, "You'll be a whore someday just like your mother."

Sharon's foster family had different expectations for their own son. He struggled in school, while Sharon was a bright girl. As a result, she became the butt of the foster mother's disappointment and frustrations. It would break Sharon's heart to listen to the boy's frustration and his mother's anger when he tried to do homework or learn spelling words. On one occasion when Sharon tried to defend the boy, the mother raged, "I hope you have a child just like him some day."

One of the most common stressors in our society is trauma from family violence and abuse. According to World Health Organization statistics on abuse and family violence, 3.2 million children every year are reported to Child Protective Services agencies as alleged victims of child maltreatment. That means that every hour as many as 115 children are being abused.

Every nine seconds, a woman in the United States is assaulted or beaten. Around the world, at least one in three women have been beaten, coerced into sex, or otherwise abused during her lifetime. Most often, the abuser is a member of her own family. Domestic violence is the leading cause of injury to women—more than car accidents, muggings and rapes combined. Studies suggest that up to ten million children every year witness some form of domestic violence and suffer physically and emotionally because of it.

Statistics like these are horrifying, yet experts tell us we are only seeing the tip of the iceberg. Based on reports from ten countries, it is believed that 55 to 95% of women who have been physically abused by their partners never contact government organizations, shelters or police for help. Domestic violence and abuse are largely hidden crimes because victims are afraid to share their disturbing experiences for fear of further or more serious abuse.

Types of abuse
Abuse can take several different forms. All of them can cause trauma and untold psychological damage.

Psychological or emotional abuse
This occurs when a person's self-worth is systematically destroyed through harassment, threats, and deprivation of all kinds. Psychological abuse can also include destruction of the victim's personal property and/or pets. This is one type of the abuse that my sister Sharon suffered.

Abusive tactics in the home
This type of abuse is a deliberate pattern of abusive tactics used by one partner in an intimate relationship to maintain power and control over the other person. It may be exploitive and violent acts of a physical, sexual, or emotional nature perpetrated by spouse against spouse, parent against child, child against parent, or sibling against sibling.

Sexual abuse
Sexual abuse is the sexual exploitation of any person who is not capable of resisting contact or who is psychologically or socially dependent upon the offender.

Physical abuse

Physical abuse can be active or passive. Active abuse involves pain and/ or damage that is deliberately inflicted by one person upon another. Passive abuse is the failure to provide the necessities of life (food, clothing, shelter, healthcare, etc.) for an individual.

Spousal abuse (wife battering)

This is the repeated subjection of a woman to any forceful physical or psychological behaviour by a man in order to coerce her to do something he wants her to do without any concern for her rights. Although there are fewer incidents of husband abuse, it does take place.

Child abuse or battered child syndrome

This is the deliberate, non-accidental injury to, sexual stimulation of, neglect of, or ridiculing of a child. This type of abuse involves exploitation and violence, and includes physical, sexual, and emotional abuse.

Characteristics of Batterers

About 50 to 80% witnessed or experienced abuse as children.

- The abuser is generally traditional in his views regarding gender roles and becomes angry if his spouse fails to comply with his expectations.
- The abuser is often introverted and non-assertive, has a low self-esteem, and poor communications skills.
- He has great difficulty trusting other people.
- Abusers have a need to be in control of their situation, and will frequently make statements like, "You are my wife and you will do what I tell you to do."
- The only emotion the abusers (both men and women) recognize is anger. Their rage and aggression give them the sense of being in control, though in reality, they are out of control.

I have experienced a number of abuses. There was definitely emotional abuse resulting from the feeling that our parents had rejected and abandoned us. While I was never physically abused by my father, I certainly witnessed physical abuse when he would attack my mother. That continued with my mom's live-in boyfriends. One, in particular, was exceedingly violent.

In the foster home, there was ongoing verbal abuse, and my brother and I were often slapped, hit in the head and strapped. To this day, I react instinctively when someone grabs me unexpectedly from behind.

The abuse was even more traumatic for my little brother. We both lived in a constant state of fear.

My sister Sharon suffered severe verbal and emotional abuse. Like my brother and me, she was deliberately deprived of emotional security. Though our mother wrote letters to her, Sharon never saw them herself. The foster mother didn't want Sharon getting the absurd idea that she was loved and remembered. Instead, she did everything she could to communicate that Sharon was unworthy, dirty, immoral and ungrateful.

One night when Sharon was about twelve, she was left alone with her foster brother while the adults played cards at a house up the street. Sharon was beginning to develop physically, and the foster brother tried to reach under her pyjama top to investigate. Sharon pushed him away and kicked him in the shins. A day or two later his mother noticed a bruise on his leg and questioned him. The boy told her Sharon kicked him. When Sharon tried to defend herself, she was attacked. She was told that the boy would never have done that, and if he was curious, it must have been because Sharon acted in some way to get his attention.

When Sharon complained another time that the boy was using a mirror to peek into her room to watch her get dressed, she was again told she was the one in the wrong, and after that was required to keep her door open at all times. Until she was eighteen years old, Sharon undressed behind a dresser in the corner of her room.

Physical Signs of Child Abuse

- The child has injuries that cannot be explained or has repeated injuries of the same kind.
- The child shows evidence of repeated skin injuries or other injuries.
- The child's injuries are inappropriately treated by means of bandages or medication.
- The child's living conditions pose a threat to good health.
- The child is kept confined, as in a crib or playpen (or even a cage) for overly long periods of time.
- The child appears to be undernourished, or is given inappropriate food, drink or medicine.
- The child is dressed inappropriately for weather conditions.
- The child shows evidence of poor care overall.
- The child seems different in terms of physical or emotional make-up and is angry. Their rage and aggression give them the sense of being in control, though in reality, they are out of control.

Why do parents abuse their children?

To understand better the path to spiritual healing, it is important to try to understand what has caused such devastating problems. Though the issues are extremely complex, research indicates that there is a high probability of child abuse in a family in situations when one or both parents experience social and emotional isolation, low self-esteem, inability to meet personal needs, inability or unwillingness to seek help, severe marital difficulties, unrealistic expectations of children, or were victims of abuse themselves.

The child may be viewed as being a problem or different from other children. This occurs most often when the child is unwanted, premature, handicapped, or born via a difficult delivery. Sometimes a child is seen as an unwelcome intrusion in the family, or as a projection of the more unacceptable qualities of the parent or another family member, or the child has special needs requiring care, attention, or effort on the part of the parent.

If there is a crisis or series of crises in the family, the conditions are there for abuse to occur. The crisis need not be major, but is experienced by the parent as personal failure, helplessness, or rejection.

Grace ran away from home at fifteen, and was now working as a waitress. She came for help to get over her fears and hatred of her past. When she was a girl, her mother drove her brothers to camp and was away overnight. Grace reported how her father crawled into her bed that night, fondled her breasts and told her he wanted her sexually.

Grace didn't say anything to her mother about the incident. In fact, she found it painful even years later to admit that her father's sexual advances had both scared and excited her. As a child she loved her father deeply and was proud of his charm and good looks, but his incestuous visits continued for three years, and as they progressed from fondling to full sexual intercourse, she grew to despise him.

One of the most prevalent forms of sexual abuse in our society is incest, or sexual intercourse between close relatives. Though it is one of the darkest stains imaginable, it is probably the most commonly concealed crime in North America today.

Consider what the Bible has to say about abuse of this kind.

The spiritual side of child abuse

In our nominally Christian culture, it is not uncommon to hear offenders using Biblical passages out of context to justify their abusive behaviour. They seek to somehow demonstrate divine sanction for their conduct by proof-texting isolated passages from scripture in an effort to rationalize what is clearly condemned by God.

We, of course, know that God the Heavenly Father does not condone child abuse of any kind. In fact, the Bible has much to say condemning child abuse.

The high worth and dignity of children

"Behold, children are a heritage from the Lord, the fruit of the womb is a reward. Like arrows in the hand of a warrior, so are the children of one's youth. Happy is the man who has his quiver full of them"(Psalm 127:3–5a).

"Then they also brought infants to Him that He might touch them, but when the disciples saw it, they rebuked them. But Jesus called them to Him and said, 'Let the little children come to Me, and do not forbid them, for of such is the kingdom of God. Assuredly I say to you, whoever does not receive the kingdom of God as a little child will by no means enter'" (Luke 18:15–17).

"Take heed that you do not despise one of these little ones" (Matthew 18:10a).

The serious judgement on parental neglect

"But if anyone does not provide for his own, and especially for those of his household, he has denied the faith and is worse than an unbeliever" (I Timothy 5:8).

"The rod and rebuke give wisdom, but a child left to himself brings shame to his mother" (Proverbs 29:15).

The condemnation of emotional abuse

"And you, fathers, do not provoke your children to wrath, but bring them up in the training and admonition of the Lord" (Ephesians 6:4).

"Fathers, do not provoke your children, lest they become discouraged" (Colossians 3:2).

An adult intentionally marring a child's moral character or development is condemned

"But whoever causes one of these little ones who believe in Me to stumble, it would be better for him if a millstone were hung around his neck, and he were thrown into the sea" (Mark 9:42).

Positive parenting is presented as a vital contribution to a child's development of positive identity and lifestyle

"The righteous man walks in his integrity; his children are blessed after him" (Proverbs 20:7).

"Train up a child in the way he should go, and when he is old he will not depart from it" (Proverbs 22:6).

Parallels are drawn between human parenting and the paternal qualities of God

"As a father pities his children, so the Lord pities those who fear Him" (Psalm 103:13).

"If you then, being evil, know how to give good gifts to your children, how much more will your heavenly Father give the Holy Spirit to those who ask Him!" (Luke 11:13).

Responsible parenting is a high and sacred calling

"...admonish the young women to love their husbands, to love their children" (Titus 2:4).

"Can a woman forget her nursing child, and not have compassion on the son of her womb?" (Isaiah 49:15a).

"The father of the righteous will greatly rejoice, and he who begets a wise child will delight in him" (Proverbs 23:24).

Sexual abuse in all forms is condemned

"But if a man finds a betrothed young woman in the countryside and the man forces her and lies with her, then only the man who lay with her shall die. But you shall do nothing to the young woman; there is in the young woman no sin deserving of death, for just as when a man rises against his neighbour and kills him, even so is this matter" (Deuteronomy 22:25-27).

"None of you shall approach anyone who is near of kin to him to uncover his nakedness" (Leviticus 18:6). The passage goes on to explain the long and specific list of close relatives who are unlawful sexual partners.

Everything we possess—including our body and our health—is on loan from God for the duration of our life time. Since our life is not merely our own, but also God's, when we are physically or sexually abused, God's property is abused and violated. The victim's hurt, anger and disappointment are shared by God.

"Or do you not know that your body is the temple of the Holy Spirit who is in you, whom you have from God, and you are not your own? For you were bought with a price; therefore glorify God in your body and in your spirit, which are God's" (1 Corinthians 6: 19, 20).

"Do you not know that you are the temple of God and that the Spirit of God dwells in you? If anyone defiles the temple of God, God will destroy him, for the temple of God is holy, which temple you are" (I Corinthians 3:16, 17).

Children are an inheritance from God, on loan to parents who are accountable for their stewardship and caretaking. Children are not owned by parents. Abuse cannot be tolerated even under the guise of discipline: "Behold, children are a heritage from the Lord, the fruit of the womb is a reward" (Psalms 127:3).

When you are the victim

Lori was a single woman who felt inferior for as long as she could remember. As a result, people took advantage of her, especially men. She was raped on more than one occasion.

Lori longed for love, security and happiness, but what she'd received was broken promises, rejection, fear, and guilt. After all she'd been through, she had a difficult time believing that Jesus could really love her.

When Lori came for counseling, there were a number of areas in her life where she needed help to find freedom. She resented her father for causing her mother to be a fearful, depressed woman. Since Lori had such a poor father image, she held similar feelings toward God. Understandably, given her past experiences, she had a difficult time trusting men in general.

As I counseled Lori, it became obvious what the stress factors were in her life. Counseling revealed problems in the areas of anxiety, depression, inhibition, subjectivity and hostility. We used God's Word to initiate a program to alleviate the stress factors in her life. Lori's homework was to go through prescribed Bible verses on fear and memorize the ones that stood out for her. Since she had not had a consistent Bible study and devotional plan, I provided one for her to use during her daily devotional time. The plan included reading one chapter of the Bible each day, writing down the theme of its contents, the key verse, and the life application lessons she gleaned from the chapter.

Lori also had to deal with the bitterness she felt toward her father. I instructed her to spend time each day praying about it. We scheduled a specific day on which she would pray for emotional healing to get rid of the memories of her traumatic childhood experiences and the rapes.

None of this was easy for Lori; she had a hard time giving up control and allowing Jesus Christ to take over every area of her life. But though her progress was slow, the results were significant. Following the prayer for emotional healing, Lori was able to be more consistent in her devotional times with God. Instead of viewing Jesus as out to punish her, she was able to accept God's love and forgiveness, and then to forgive herself. Lori conceded that as long as she was consistent with the Bible study pattern of content, key verse and lessons learned, she was not depressed or fearful. She also had a better view of Jesus Christ as the One who loved her.

Lori's self-esteem grew more positive; she gained emotional stability and security, and became more open with and comfortable around Christian men. She eventually married a fine Christian gentleman and they both became involved in ministry.

Why me?

Trauma and abuse are a sad reality in our fallen world. One of the questions people often ask is, "Why me?" Everyone asking that question needs to know they are not alone.

Jesus, the most pivotal person in the Bible, also asked a "why" question. Knowing He was going to die a horrible, agonizing death, He asked, "Father, why have you forsaken Me?" Even though Jesus was the Son of God—and knew beyond a shadow of doubt there was an ultimate and glorious purpose for His unjust death—He still asked the deeply human question, "Why?"

There is no end to those questions, nor are there any really satisfying answers. Jesus once told his closest friends, "In this world you will have trouble, but take heart for I have overcome the world" (John 16:33). Jesus was speaking of a long-term plan, a plan where He and His Father will ultimately destroy suffering and evil. They will create a new heaven and a new earth and the old, ugly, painful experiences of the past will be gone forever. This new place will be one of peace, and fulfillment, and joy in God's presence.

If deep pain and trauma have been your experience, you may be saying, "Sorry, that's not good enough for me right now." Take heart.

More than anything else, you need to know that you are loved deeply and passionately by God who, if you choose Him, will someday lift away the suffering and evil that has invaded your life. The Bible says that God is "gracious and compassionate, slow to anger and abounding in love." Know that even in the midst of your emotional pain, God is looking upon you with compassion and love.

Here are some steps you can take to help yourself on the journey to spiritual healing. Remember there is a Creator God who loves you and that even though He may not remove the pain quickly or entirely, He wants to walk with you through this suffering. Understand that God has a good plan for your life. "For I know the thoughts that I think toward you, says the Lord, thoughts of peace and not of evil, to give you a future and a hope" (Jeremiah 29:11). Because of this, a good first step in dealing with the pain of trauma and abuse is to pray. You might pray like this: Dear God, I hurt. Sometimes the pain is so overwhelming I can't seem to get my breath. But I've read that You love me and have compassion toward me. I've learned that You see my pain and want to walk me through it. I pray that You will take away my memories, my fears, my physical reactions to the things I've experienced, my distance from family and friends, and the worry that I will never be normal again. I want to live a full life; I want to live the life You've planned for me. Help me find practical and spiritual ways to overcome the evil and suffering on this earth so that I can live in joy and peace and find your fulfillment in my life. Thank You for hearing my prayer."

You may find healing almost immediately, or you may merely begin your healing journey with this prayer. It is important that you pray daily, while you learn the skills you need to heal. I don't know the plans God has for you, but I know He has them, and that He wants to show His compassion to you.

Take time to exercise, even if at first it's only walking around the block. If being outside alone makes you too fearful, walk around your living space or climb stairs. Daily exercise helps to relieve some of the symptoms of stress and fear. Try to eat a healthy diet, even if eating feels too hard sometimes. A diet with plenty of fruits and vegetables, along with low-fat protein sources, is important. Avoid caffeine, nicotine, and unnatural sugars which may increase feelings of anxiety and hyper-arousal. A friend, a Christian medical doctor, encourages his patients to do deep breathing exercises, that would help them. He suggests to breathe deeply through your nose while filling your diaphragm (below your rib cage). Slowly release the air through your mouth. It is especially important to practice deep-breathing when you are feeling tense, after having a flashback, before you go to sleep, or when you're in an anxiety-provoking situation.

There is no need for you to recount every specific detail of the trauma or traumas you have experienced. Well-meaning but misinformed counselors may attempt to have you relay all the horrors you've endured in one telling. Doing so can lead to re-traumatisation. There may come a time to discuss all that transpired, but this should be done only with a trained, qualified professional who is able to prepare and support you in the process. Staying locked inside your home is not an ideal solution for overcoming traumatic events. There may be occasions when it is necessary to travel near or go past a specific place where something traumatic happened, or encounter a person who hurt you. When this happens, it is vitally important to fortify yourself with prayer and use Scripture verses to help you through the stress.

God has given us a wonderful tool in the form of our imagination. Using the imagination to help you feel 'normal,' even for a few seconds, is extremely helpful. Find a place that is quiet and peaceful. Sit or stand comfortably. Take a few deep breaths. Feel your feet on the floor, or your back against the chair, and breathe deeply a few more times.

Let your memory go back to a time when you felt normal, fulfilled, or at peace especially in your relationship with Jesus Christ. Do not let your mind wander into self-pity where you bemoan your current fate. Rather, recall what it felt like to feel normal or at peace. What did it smell like? Look like? Taste like? Get your senses involved as much as possible to create a vivid experience.

Allow yourself a few minutes for this, reliving these specific memories as clearly as you can. Keep breathing deeply. You need opportunities to feel normal and for some people, the easiest and safest way is by *carefully* using their imagination.

If intrusive flashbacks attempt to disrupt you, go back to deep breathing, focus on your feet touching the floor or your back against the chair, the smell of the room, a picture on the wall. Once you've finished, try praying some of the following prayers out loud while maintaining the deep-breathing: "Dear God, I have just read that You are gracious and compassionate, that You have great love for me. I'm in need of compassion and love right now. I pray that I will sense Your trustworthy and loving presence even as I pray. I've also read that You have a plan for my life, a hope and a future. Some days I'm so haunted by feelings of doom that this seems impossible to me. However, I want to believe it. I want You to fulfill good things in my life. I ask that You will start doing that right now, even as I pray. Thank You for hearing me."

Or: "It says in the Bible, 'Because of the Lord's great love we are not consumed, for His compassions never fail. They are new every morning; great is your faithfulness. I say to myself, "The Lord is my portion; therefore I will wait for him." The Lord is good to those whose hope is in Him, to the one who seeks Him; it is good to wait quietly for the salvation of the Lord' (Lamentations 3:22-26). I admit I haven't been looking for your mercies every morning, but I pray that I will begin to, God. I desperately need hope right now and this passage says You are that hope. I don't feel very trusting, but I need to take some small steps, so please hear this prayer and answer me. Thank You, Lord, that You are good. Help me experience what good looks and feels like."

In Psalm 107 there are vivid pictures of people in all kinds of difficulty. What they have in common is that ". . .they cried out to the Lord in their trouble and He saved them from their distress." Please, God, save me from my distress. "I want to 'cast my cares' on you, Lord, and have you sustain me" (Psalm 55:22).

God is closer than you imagine. He wants to help carry your sorrow and suffering.

Christ's healing for our pain and brokenness

It is nearly impossible to live in confidence if we carry heavy burdens of hurts and scars from our past. Everyone has some hurts because we live in a fallen world. All our hurts and problems are unique to us. I may have thirty people in a seminar on abuse, but every person's situation will be unique. We choose how we will respond to and how we will cope with our pain. Three of my brothers became alcoholics; my mom and dad died because of their alcoholism. It was their choice. The better choice, and the choice that results in victory over our pain and brokenness is to seek answers and guidance for living from the Bible. Let me share a testimony of two of my clients, a pastor and his wife, who were subjected to years of spiritual abuse. They continue to work through the Biblical principles that I shared with them for their emotional, mental and spiritual healing and desire to use these spiritual principles in their ongoing ministry.

"When Jesus began His ministry He quoted Isaiah saying, "I have come to bind up the broken hearted and to set the captives free". We have learned through Bruce's teaching and counsel that 'emotional healing' is how Jesus binds up our broken hearts. We had always believed that when we became new creations in Christ we were no longer to dwell on or acknowledge the past or its effects on us. We thought, "It's over, we should move on." However, we have learned that it was impossible to "move on" without learning how to forgive and apply the power of Jesus Christ's death and resurrection to those moments in our lives that had continued to affect the way we were living, believing and thinking.

Bruce listened and encouraged us through prayer, God's Word and godly counsel. All the while he said that he was "excited" about how God was transforming us into new creations. At times the pain was so great we could not see how we would come through it all, but Bruce became God-in-skin to us, walking in love, giving us hope. We now hope to live out our ministry to help bring emotional healing to those that Christ puts in our path."

As well as learning how to counsel through the power of the Holy Spirit, I am indebted to the many authors and speakers who have given us Biblical principles to gain victory in our lives and the lives of thousands of individuals.

Consider some of these principles by Charles Mylander and others, as you continue on your journey to mental, emotional and spiritual healing:

1. Set your mind on the presence and power of Christ.

I do this in my personal life by sharing God's Word back to Him. Early each morning as I meet with Almighty God, I deliberately focus on His presence and power.

"But seek first the kingdom of God and His righteousness, and all these things will be added to you" (Matthew 6:3).

2. Ask for the Holy Spirit's cleansing and filling daily.

As we make this a daily practice, we can walk in God's victory.

"But if we walk in the light as He is in the light, we have fellowship with one another, and the blood of Jesus Christ His Son cleanses us from all sin" (1 John 1:7).

"And do not be drunk with wine, in which is dissipation, but be filled with the Spirit" (Ephesians 5:18).

3. Be armed for spiritual battle to resist the enemy.

My daily practise is to quote Ephesians 6:10-18 and apply that to my life and to my family's life.

"Finally, brethren, be strong in the Lord and in the power of His might. Put on the whole armor of God that you may be able to stand against the wiles of the devil. For we do not wrestle against flesh and blood, but against principalities, against powers, against the rulers of the darkness of this age, against spiritual hosts of wickedness in the heavenly places. Therefore take up the whole armour of God, that you may be able to withstand in the evil day, and having done all, to stand" (Ephesians 6: 10-13).

4. Memorize scripture.

God has given me this desire over the years to memorize scripture to quote as I counsel and pray for individuals. The power of God's Word has given individuals freedom.

"This Book of the Law shall not depart from your mouth, but you shall meditate in it day and night that you may observe to do according to all that is written in it. For then you will make your way prosperous and then you will have good success" (Joshua 1:8).

"For the word of God is living and powerful, and sharper than any two-edged sword, piercing even to the division of the soul and spirit, and of joints and marrow, and is a discerner of the thoughts and intents of the heart" (Hebrews 4:12).

5. Ask God for a hatred of sin.

As a child of God and as a counselor I ask the Holy Spirit to point out sin in my life so I can confess and repent of it.

"Do you not know that your body is the temple of the Holy Spirit who is in you, whom you have from God, and you are not your own? For you were bought at a price, therefore glorify God in your body and in your spirit, which are God's" (1 Corinthians 6:19, 20).

"I have been crucified with Christ; it is no longer I who live, but Christ lives in me; and the life which I now live in the flesh I live by faith in the Son of God, who loved me and gave Himself for me" (Galatians 2:20).

6. Know your besetting sin and be on guard.

Every one of us as believers have two or three sinful areas that we continue to struggle with. It may be pride, self-pity, anger, lust, fear, resentment, etc. We must call it sin when we give in to it and ask God to forgive us and remove it from our lives. As often as we fall, be spiritually aggressive and give it to Christ.

"For you, brethren, have been called to liberty; only do not use liberty as an opportunity for the flesh, but through love serve one another. For all the law is fulfilled in one word, even in this: 'You shall love your neighbour as yourself.' But if you bite and devour one another, beware lest you be consumed by one another" (Galatians 5:13-15).

7. Develop a life of praise to God.

Each day as we meet with God, make it a point to worship and praise God. We can use Scripture passages, hymns, choruses, poems, etc. to exalt our Lord.

"Make a joyful shout to the Lord, all you lands! Serve the Lord with gladness; come before His presence with singing. Know that the Lord, He is God; it is He who has made us, and not we ourselves. We are His people and the sheep of His pasture. Enter into His gates with thanksgiving and into His courts with praise. Be thankful to Him and bless His name. For the Lord is good; His mercy is everlasting, and His truth endures to all generations" (Psalm 100:1-5).

8. Expect to resolve conflicts as you obey Christ.

Since God promised that He would never leave us nor forsake us, we can be confident that we can resolve conflicts that press upon us. We must recognise of course that His thoughts and ways are not always what we might wish. In Isaiah 55 we read: 'For My thoughts are not your thoughts, Nor are your ways My ways,' says the LORD. 'For as the heavens are higher than the earth, So are My ways higher than your ways, And My thoughts than your thoughts' (Isaiah 55:8, 9).

Jesus shared, ". . .and lo, I am with you always, even to the end of the age. Amen" (Matt. 28:20).

"If you had known Me, you would have known My Father also; and from now on you know Him and have seen Him" (John 14:7).

"I can do all things through Christ who strengthens me . . . And my God shall supply all your need according to His riches in glory by Christ Jesus" (Phil. 4:13, 19).

Here are more scripture passages to consider:

Romans 8:31–39	Psalm 139:1–18
Matthew 11:28–30	Hebrews 4:12–18
John 8: 31, 32, 36	Psalm 23:1–6

My sister Sharon is a wonderful example of how God's Word, put into practise, could set her free from a painful childhood, a traumatic divorce and the challenges as a single parent. I will give Sharon the final word on healing:

"How hard it is to believe that over fifty years have passed since my time in a foster home. When you are living in a situation like that you begin to believe that it will last forever! Once released from that overly structured and demeaning environment, I was on my own to learn and make good and sometimes bad choices, as we all do in life. There were many struggles, failures, accomplishments and both happy and sad times. During all this time I have nurtured my faith and my faith has nurtured and sustained me. Romans 8:28 has been an important verse for me. I am now a retired teacher with a husband who is very kind and treats me with love and respect. My children are close to me and I feel very blessed. I still keep in touch with my foster brother who has lived on his own for the last 14 years and loves sharing with me. I truly thank God who has given me the strength and wisdom to endure and rejoice in His abundance."

Bibliography and Guide for Further Reading

Through the years—and through the writing of this book—I have been indebted to the work and scholarship of many authors, publishing houses and, increasingly, websites. These excellent resources help all of us who are broken (and that is probably all of us) seek healing through spiritual counseling. Throughout the book, I have referenced many works, which I list again below.

Ahlem, L. (1973). *Do I Have To Be Me?* Glendale: Gospel Light.

Augsburger, D. (1973). *The Freedom of Forgiveness.* Chicago: Moody Press.

Bounds, E. M. (1976). *The Necessity of Prayer.* Grand Rapids: Baker Book House.

Brown, R. (1986). *He Came to Set the Captives Free.* Chino: Chick.

Bubeck, M. I. (1975). *The Adversary.* Chicago: Moody Press.

Carlson, D. (1981). *Overcoming Hurts and Anger.* Eugene: Harvest House.

Carr, L. & Carr, G. (1990). *The Fierce Goodbye.* Downers Grove: InterVarsity Press.

Chapman, G. (1999). *Anger: Handling a Powerful Emotion in a Healthy Way.* Grand Rapids: Zondervan.

Collins, G. (1972). *Effective Counseling.* Illinois: Creation House.

Conway, S. (1984). *You and Your Husband's Mid-Life Crisis.* Weston: David C. Cook.

Comstock, G., Chaffee, S., Katzman, N., McCombs, M. & Roberts, D. (1978). *Television and Human Behavior.* New York: Columbia University Press.

Dobson, J. (1978). *The Strong-willed Child.* Wheaton: Tyndale House.

Dobson, J. (1983). *Love Must Be Tough.* Waco: Word Books.

Doka, K. J. (Ed.). (1996). *Living with Grief After Sudden Loss.* The Hospice Foundation of America.

Eastman, D. & Hayford, J. (1988). *Living and Praying in Jesus' Name.* Wheaton: Tyndale House.

Edwards, J. (1978). *The Life of David Brainerd.* Grand Rapids: Baker Book House.

Flach, F. (2009). *The Secret Strength of Depression.* Hobart: Hatherleigh Press.

Forward, S. (1988). *A Betrayal of Innocence.* New York: Penguin.

Frangipane, F. (1989). *The Three Battlegrounds.* Marion: Advancing Church Publications.

Frank, J. (1987). *Door of Hope.* San Bernardino: Here's Life.

Frank, J. (1990). *Why Victims Marry.* San Bernardino: Here's Life.

Fischer, T. F. (2004). *The Ministry Of Rejection: Number 297.* Support and Resources for Pastors and Christian Ministry Professionals.

Gil, E. (1983). *Outgrowing the Pain Together.* New York: Dell.

Grollman, E. A. (1974). *Concerning Death: A Practical Guide for Living.* Boston: Beacon Press.

Haggai, J. (2001). *How to Win Over Worry.* Eugene: Harvest House.

Harvey, V. (2000). *Psychology for Living.* Narramore Christian Foundation. Retrieved from http://www.ncfliving.org/eating_disorders1.php

Hart, A. *Depression.* Focus on the Family. Retrieved from http://www.focusonthefamily.com/lifechallenges/emotional_health/depression.aspx

Hawkins, D. & Pauling L. (1973). *Orthomolecular Psychiatry.* San Francisco: W. H. Freeman.

Hendricks, H. (1974). *Heaven Help the Home.* Wheaton: Victor Books.

Heitritter, L. & Vought, J. (1989). *Helping Victims of Sexual Abuse.* Minneapolis: Bethany House.

Hunt, J. (2007). *Freedom through Forgiveness: Hope from the Heart.* Eugene: Harvest House.

Johnson, W. C. (September 1982). Demon Possession and Mental Illness. *The American Scientific Affiliation.* Retrieved from http://www.asa3.org/ASA/PSCF/1982/JASA9-82Johnson.html

Katz, W. (1983). *Protecting Your Child From Sexual Assault*. Toronto: Little Ones Books.

Koch, K. (1970). *Occult, Bondage and Deliverance*. Grand Rapids: Kregal.

Koop, C. E. (1976). *The Right to Live; The Right to Die*. Wheaton: Tyndale House.

LaHaye, T. & LaHaye, B. (1976). *The Act of Marriage*. Grand Rapids: Zondervan.

Leman, K. (2007). *Why Your Best Is Good Enough*. Grand Rapids: Revell Baker.

Lutzer, E. W. (1975). *Failure, the Backdoor to Success*. Chicago: Moody Press.

Markell, J. (1982). *Overcoming Stress*. Wheaton: Victor Books.

McDowell, J. (2012). *Undaunted*. Campus Crusade for Christ: Tyndale House.

Minirth, F., Meier, P. & Hawkins, D. (1992). *The Stress Factor*. Chicago: Northfield.

Mylander, C. (1986). *Running the Red Lights*. Ventura: Regal Books.

Narramore, B. (1978). *You're Some Special*. Grand Rapids: Zondervan.

Timmons, T. (1976). *Maximum Marriage*. Grand Rapids: Fleming H. Revell.

Scazzero, P. (2006). *Emotionally Healthy Spirituality*. Nashville: Thomas Nelson.

Seamands, D. A. (1981). *Healing For Damaged Emotions.* Wheaton: Victor Books.

Solomon, C. R. (1999). *Handbook to Happiness.* Wheaton: Tyndal.

Tapscott, B. (1975). *Inner Healing Through Healing of Memories.* Houston: Hunter Books.

Wagner, C. P. (1991). *Territorial Spirits.* Chichester: Richard Clay.

Walsh, S. (2004). *The Heartache No One Sees.* Nashville: Thomas Nelson.

Warner, T. H. (1991). *Spiritual Warfare.* Wheaton: Crossway Books.

White, J. (1982). *The Masks of Melancholy.* Downers Grove: InterVarsity Press.

White, T. B. (1990). *The Believer's Guide to Spiritual Warfare.* Ann Harbour: Servant.

Wiese, B. R. & Steinmentz, G. U. (1972). *Everything You Need to Know to Stay Married and Like It.* Grand Rapids: Zondervan.

Wilkerson, D. (1978). *Suicide.* Old Tappan: Fleming H. Revell.

Williams, P. (1973). *Do Yourself A Favor: Love Your Wife.* Plainfield: Logos International.

Wolfelt, A. (1990). *A Child's View of Grief.* Fort Collins: Companion Press.

Wolfelt, A. (2011). *Center for Loss & Life Transition.* www.centerforloss.com

Wright, N. (1980). *The Pillars of Marriage.* Venture: Gospel Light.

Wright, N. (1982). *The Healing of Fears.* Eugene: Harvest House.

Printed in Canada